CONTINUOUS IMPROVEMENT

THE LEAN WAY

MOHIT SHARMA

Qurate
qauratebooks.com
Because everyone has a story to tell

CONTINUOUS IMPROVEMENT
THE LEAN WAY
Mohit Sharma

Published by Qurate Books Pvt. Ltd.

First Published in 2023

ISBN: 978-93-94600-65-2

qurate
quratebooks.com
Because everyone has a story to tell

Qurate Books Pvt. Ltd.
Goa 403523, India
www.quratebooks.com
Tel: 1800-210-6527, Email: info@quratebooks.com

Printed at Manipal Technologies Limited, Manipal

Table Of Contents

Preface:

Quality is not an act, it is a habit. This book helps readers to develop quality work as a habit.

It explains all the lean tools in the beginning and then gives the reader 8 step quality methodology. The methodology is important to drive continuous improvement culture in an Organisation. The attempt here is to teach the readers how to identify continuous improvement projects and how to get them to closure. What are the different roadblocks that are faced during the projects and how they can be overcome?

There are four case studies which help the reader to learn the implementation of tools and lean methodology in different industry situations.

1. Increase email response rate could be a problem for any Organisation - be it services or manufacturing. This case study helps the user to learn how to dissect the business problem into actionable solutions and how to use data to take and validate actions.
2. Reduce turnaround time of invoice processing in Finance and accounting process is an important goal across industries. All companies whether manufacturing or services have Finance and accounting function and on time processing of invoices is important to run a hassle-free business. This case study helps the reader in identifying that how change in physical layout of the process can help improve team's efficiency. The role of automation and robotics is immensely important in the modern times and the case study is the excellent example of their implementation.
3. Third case study talks about cycle time reduction of a software development process and is a very good example for software business to understand the application of lean in their industry.

As all business problems are identified by listening to customer's escalations / issues so is with the software business. This case study emphasizes on the fact of understanding customer's requirement upfront, putting governances around the processes and data usage to identify the root causes to the problems. This case study will also help the readers to understand the application of the complex concepts of lean like Heijunka, Kaizen and Jidokha in software industry. It also helps them learn, how to identify the failure modes of the new solution implementations and mitigate with the help of FMEA analysis.

4. To reduce the loan approval cycle time is a banking sector case study which helps the readers to understand the reasons of delay in loan processing and how lean tools can help identify those reasons. This case explains the need of identifying the problem clearly upfront and usage of tools like value stream mapping in identifying the non-value-added activities and steps. This example explains the use of Kano Model and its implementation.

All the above case studies explain the importance of control plan / control charts and how important it is to control the improved state of the process to avoid failures.

There is a difference in doing a project and mentoring someone who is doing a project. This book also provides a unique learning experience of how to mentor lean projects. Mentoring guide explains what all tools and methods are to be used during all 8-step methodology, what are the various dos and don'ts at each stage of the project, etc.

All in all, this book is a complete guide on implementing lean tools and methodology in any work area. I wish the readers all the best.

What is Lean?

Definition:

Lean is a principle driven, tools-based philosophy that focuses on eliminating waste so that all activities/steps add value from the customers perspective.

There are 5 principles of Lean, 20+ tools and 8 types of wastes which exists. We need to identify & eliminate these wastes with the help of various lean principles and tools, thereby creating a system / process that will add value from customer's perspective.

Let us first learn what does value add mean from customer's perspective

Value add activity can be referred to any activity which meets the following three criterias:

- There should be some form of change.
- It should be done right the first time.
- Customer should be ready to pay for it.

Apart from the above value-add activities, there are some essential non-value add (enablers) activities which cannot be eliminated altogether, and rest are pure non-value activities.

Form of change – E.g.: Service request changing into an invoice, Request changing into credit issued etc.

Done right first time – This has more to do with the inverse that auditing, monitoring and checking are all no value add.

Ready to pay – This means that the customer agrees that the activity is required and essential. E.g.: customer requires error free products or services and if we put a quality check team then customer will not pay us for those resources. It becomes non-value-added activity. We are supposed to do things right in the first go and customer will not pay us for our errors, so it is non-value-added activity. In a situation when customer says that they want 100% audit for the products they are receiving, and they are willing to pay for the resources cost, then in this case it becomes value-added activity.

Lean Principles:

There are 5 main lean principles which are as follows:

1. Specify the Value from Customer's perspective
2. Map the Value stream
3. Establish the flow
4. Implement pull
5. Work towards perfection

1. Specify Value from Customer's perspective: If we do not listen to our end customer, then we are living in a fool's paradise where we will feel that we are working well, and customers are happy with what we produce. Whereas in reality customers would feel uncared for and move to our competition where they feel they are heard and cared for.

So, understand what your customer wants and deliver as per their expectations. Don't forget your organisation's interest we well. Best tool to study this is VOC / VOB tool (Voice of Customer and Voice of Business tool)

2. Map the Value stream: Identify all the steps currently required to move products from order to delivery i.e. from start to end of a service.

Assign the values like cycle time, wait time and first pass yield to the defined steps. This will help you to identify non-value-added steps and will help you remove them from the system.

3. Establish the flow: Line up all steps that truly create value in a rapid sequence or in other words optimize the flow of information/value across the steps.

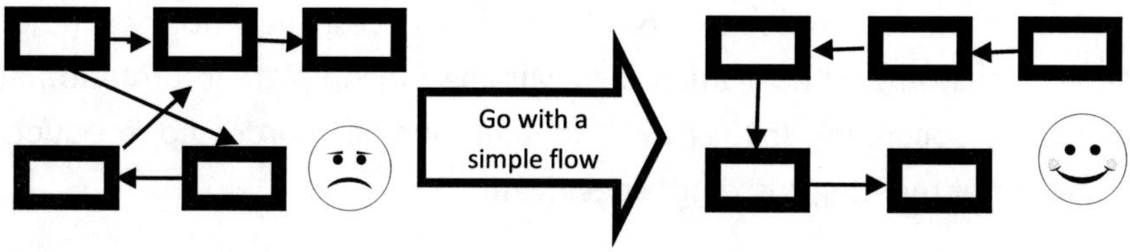

4. Implement Pull: Create a process where production happens on the request of the downstream process i.e. to replenish the inventory used by downstream process.

Let's look at an example from the car manufacturing industry. Auto companies were earlier working on Push system where cars were manufactured and stored in the warehouses which at times resulted in a lot of inventory. Then if a model was not sold in the same year, then the companies offered huge discounts to dispose it off. Models which were never sold had to be scrapped eventually. The companies finally realized the problem with the Push system and shifted over to Pull production where they first receive the order and then they start the production. So, in Pull production customer as a downstream process pulls the products.

5. Work towards perfection: Continuous improvement and innovation in existing & new products and services will lead to better outputs. As LEAN methodology says, "You cannot reach perfection, but the journey towards perfection yields continuous improvements."

Lean Wastes:

Waste is any step or action that does not add value to the final product or service. It is a step that is NOT required to complete the process successfully.

When waste is eliminated, it increases output, reduces down time and we gain more time to perform value added activities.

There are mainly 8 type of wastes:

- **Defects**: These are products / services that do not meet customer specification e.g.: Missing / incomplete information in a document, Invoice with missing purchase order no, products not meeting customer specification.

- **Overproduction**: This happens when production is more than the demand. E.g.: if the human resource department hires 13 new employees when there is work for 12 only, they have overproduced. It has increased the inventory of the resources which basically means that the additional resource would end up sitting "on bench" till the HR department finds a job for him/her.

- **Waiting**: This is the time spent in waiting for the result of the previous step. e.g.: Waiting for a cab in the morning, waiting outside Doctor's chamber for your turn, waiting in the bank queue, waiting for report in the process, waiting for approval email from manager.

- **Not utilizing talent**: This happens when employees / machines are not utilized at their full potential. E.g.: A charted accountant working in a data entry job, a laptop being used only as a calculator.

- **Transportation**: It is when waste is created due to unnecessary transportation of products and material. E.g.: A product is supposed to move from position A to B. However, it takes a complete circle of the manufacturing unit before reaching point B. This could be due to bad layout of the unit. Unnecessary transportation could lead to damaged products and hence should be avoided.

- **Inventory**: This could be excess raw material due to maintaining more-than-minimum inventory levels. E.g.: Fresh breads availability in the supermarket. If supermarket don't plan their inventory well and have extra stock, then bread will not be fresh after a day or so and customers will not buy stale bread. If they under plan and stock less quantity, then they could lose the opportunity to make a sale due to unavailability of bread. So, accurate forecasting is very important to plan right inventory level.

- **Motion waste**: This is due to unnecessary movement of human beings. E.g.: When an employee is not able to block nearby meeting rooms and instead has to travel 5 floors to conduct a meeting, it leads to motion waste. Motion waste leads to fatigue and low productivity.

- **Extra processing**: When an activity is not necessary to produce a functioning product or service, it is termed at extra processing. E.g.: two employees working on the same report, paint shop worker doing an extra coat of paint on the car doors etc....

Acronym to remember 8 wastes is **DOWNTIME**.

Identifying waste in daily life activities:

Suppose a person has to visit a doctor to consult about his/her bad throat and decides to visit a doctor who is in another city. The flow would look something like the below:

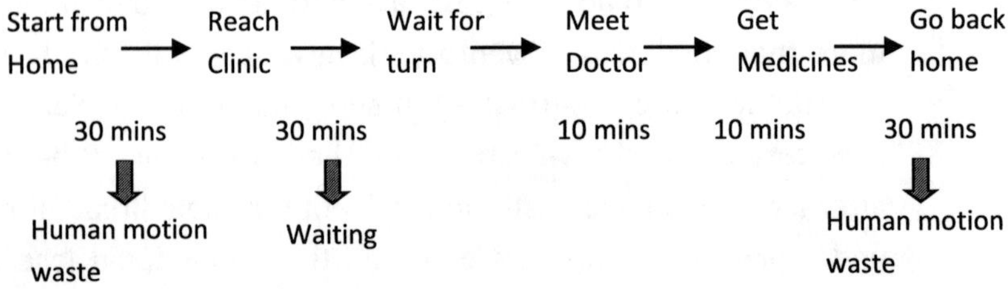

If you look at the flow chart, then identifying waste would be easy. A good doctor was also available in the same locality where the person was staying, so he/she could have avoided motion waste. A prior appointment could have further saved the waiting waste of 30 mins, so on and so forth.

Waste Category	Office Example
Over Production	Printing paperwork out before it is really needed. Purchasing items before they are needed. Processing before the next person is ready for it.
Inventory	Batch processing - transactions or reports. Files waiting to be processed.
Waiting	System downtime, system response time, approvals from others.
Extra Processing	Extra copies, unnecessary or excessive reports / transactions
Defects	Order entry errors, invoice errors. Any other error leading to rework
Motion	Walking to/from copier, fax machine in other office buildings
Transportation	Excessive email attachment, multiple hand offs.
Not Utilizing Talent	Limited employee authority & responsibility for basic task, inadequate business tools available.

5S

5S is the name of a workplace organization methodology that focuses on organizing work place so that work can be performed effectively, efficiently and safely. 5S uses a list of five Japanese words which translated into English, start with the letter S.

The term 5S comes from these five Japanese words:

- Seiri
- Seiton
- Seiso
- Seiketsu
- Shitsuke

In English, these words are translated as:

- Sort
- Set in Order
- Shine
- Standardize
- Sustain

Objective of each S is as follows:

Seiri - Sorting and Prioritizing: Going through all the tools, materials, etc., in the work area and keeping only the essential items. Everything else is stored or discarded.

Seiton - Straighten or Set in Order: Focuses on efficiency by arranging the tools, equipment, visual dashboards and parts in a manner that promotes work flow. For everything there should be place and everything should be in its place.

Seisō - Shining or Cleanliness: Systematic cleaning or the need to keep the workplace clean as well as neat. At the end of each shift, the work area is cleaned up and everything is restored to its place.

Seiketsu - Standardizing: Standardized work practices or operating in a consistent and standardized fashion. Everyone knows exactly what his or her responsibilities are to keep the above 3S's.

Shitsuke - Sustaining the discipline: Refers to maintaining and reviewing standards. Once the previous 4S's have been established, they become the new way to operate.

Let's take an example from services industry.

One of the implementations of 5S reduced the time to generate a report from 3 hours to 10 minutes.

Step 1: Sorting of data - Finance team used to generate a report which had data from 2010 till date. But the team only required data for last 1 year to do the analysis. The logic / code used to collect the historical data was modified and it reduced the overall report generation time.

Step 2: Set in order – The team needed data in a particular order for performing the analysis and hence team preset all the columns in that particular order. It helped in saving the analysis time.

Step 3: Shine – The entire report was formatted and cleaned whereby redundant rows and columns were removed. This speeded up the report generation time.

Step 4: Standardize – The report used to run during the day and it used to take lot of productivity time of both the employee and machine. But later on a standardize process was created around the time of report generation. Now every morning before the shift starts, one person runs the report for 10 minutes.

Step 5: Sustain: All the activities described above were sustained for last 3 months and now it is business as usual for the team.

Poka yoke / Mistake Proofing

Poka-yoke is a Japanese term that means "mistake-proofing". A poka-yoke is any mechanism in a Lean manufacturing process that helps an equipment operator avoid mistakes. Objective of 'Poke Yoke' is to prevent defects from happening or if they happen, prevent them from being passed to the downstream process.

Mistakes can be known at one of the following stages:

1.) Before they occur (Prediction or prevention)

2.) After they occur (Detection)

Prevention type of mistake proofing: In this mistake proofing technique, it is identified well in advance that a defect is about to happen, and it is prevented. E.g.: Asterisk sign on the web forms (if certain information is mandatory in the form and you have not filled that, you will not be able to submit that form online), access cards allow only authorised person to enter a restricted area, ATM passwords (one can't withdraw money from ATM by using some other password which is not aligned with the card.)

Detection type of mistake proofing: In this type of mistake proofing, defect is identified and stopped before it is passed on to the end customer. But we are allowing the defect to happen in this case. For example, fire alarms – they identify the fire once it is there i.e. they can detect only after the fire has started.

When to use mistake proofing: It should be used when a repeatable process is manually performed and can cause bigger defects or losses later in the production / service. The key is that process should be repeatable in nature.

How to do mistake proofing?

- Create a flow chart of the process and identify all the manual and repeatable steps.

- By looking at the budget and other details in the process, identify most critical steps where mistake proofing can be implemented.
- Identify the root cause of the potential error points.
- Identify the type of solution that can be built on that error point. It could be preventive or detective type of mistake proofing solution that can be thought of based on nature of the process and other budgetary constraints.
- Preventive type of mistake proofing would need complete automation of error point whereas detection type of mistake proofing could be done by creating audit checks at error points. A group of quality assurance resources can check sample of the cases to set up detection type of mistake proofing.

Example of Poka yoke:

In a conventional organisation where accounts payable process is totally manual:

Step 1: Invoice received manually	Step 2: Enter Invoice in System	Step3: At month end pay vendor	Step 4: Attach physical receipt

Complete Poka yoke will reduce all the manual efforts and errors created by the above process.

Step 1: Electronic invoice received	Step 2: Auto enter in system (oracle)	Step 3: Auto Pick during payment run	Step 4: Online Wire transfer

Visual Management: Visual management is one of the simplest and effective tool of lean manufacturing and Toyota production system. It is the practice of making all standards, targets and actual conditions highly visible in the workplace so that everyone can see and understand the actual conditions vs. requirements.

The key note here is that visual management is an alert mechanism, either letting us know when the fault is about to happen or when it has happened. It may be called the visual interface of any Poke yoke activity that you might have done. E.g.: In a completely automated conveyor belt setup where there is a preventive mistake proofing mechanism setup at all the machines, the machine will stop before producing any defect and a bulb will start flashing at the point where the mistake was about to happen, making it easier for the operator to identify the spot and fix the issue. This is visual management of defects.

There is no use of having metrics on the visual tool which cannot be controlled or have no significance to the end customer. Then they will just merely be numbers with no clear indicator as how / where to process the breakdown.

How to create an effective dashboard?

An effective dashboard is created with the help of the following metrics:

- Input
- Process
- Output
- Input metrics are important for us to do correct and timely work. These inputs would be output metrics for your upstream process. For e.g.: if you need data before performing your task, then you should set a timeline for that, say before 8:30 AM every day. If it is not received on time, then it should be reported in the dashboard to all the stake holders.
- Process metrics: Customer is not worried about how the team performs its task, they only need their products accurately and on time. So, some of the process metrics should be decided and

monitored as part of the dashboard. For e.g.: productivity of the team members, absenteeism and attrition.

- Output metrics: These are the metrics which are required to deliver high quality products and services. For e.g.: on-time delivery and accuracy.

In a nutshell, Visual management means managing things visually.

Some of the day-to-day examples of visual management are:

- Traffic lights,
- Signboards
- Fuel indicator in the car

Let us take an example of accounts payable process and understand how a dashboard can be prepared by using input, process and output metrics.

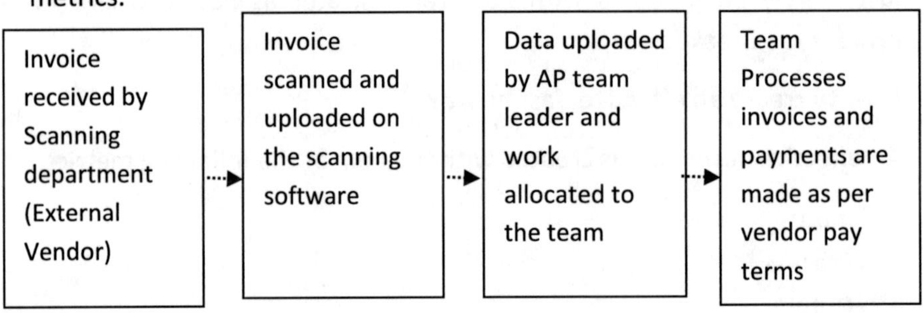

Account Payable Process

Input Metrics	Process Metrics	Output Metrics
Scanned Invoice Accuracy	Team productivity / Cycle time to process an invoice	Turnaround time
On time scanned invoices	Absenteeism in team	Accuracy of output
Vendor System uptime	Total resource working hours	No of on hold invoices greater than 30 days
	Attrition in the team	

No	Metric Name	Type of Metric	Operational Definition	Formula	Target	Data source
1	Scanned invoice accuracy	Input	Invoice received from the vendor and scanned by the scanning department. These invoices should be properly scanned and visible.	No of invoices clearly scanned / Total No of Invoices received	99.5%	Scanning software
2	On time scanned invoices	Input	Scanned Invoices should be uploaded before 8:30 AM daily	No of days invoices available on time / Total no of days	99.5%	System upload time from scanning software
3	Team productivity	Process	No of Invoices processed by the team members every day	Total No of invoices processed each day by each employee	40 each day	Allocation tool
4	Turnaround time	Output	Process the invoice as per terms defined with the Vendors	No if Invoices processed on time / Total no of invoices processed	99.5%	Reports from Oracle database
5	Accuracy of output	Output	Invoice to be processed accurately and vendor to receive correct payment	No of correctly processes invoices / Total no of invoices processed	99.97 %	Quality check report and vendor escalations

This is how one needs to define the project metrics and then create a dashboard to visually monitor the health of the process.

Just in time: Just-in-time (JIT) is an inventory strategy that strives to improve a business's return on investment by reducing in-process inventory and the associated carrying costs. To meet JIT objectives, the process relies on signals or Kanban between different points in the process, which inform the production team when to make the next part. If it is implemented correctly, JIT can dramatically improve a manufacturing organization's return on investment, quality, and efficiency.

Most of the companies that follow JIT have to acquire lot of land, not for production but for their main suppliers also to set up their plants there. This is done to ensure that the suppliers can also produce as required on the JIT principle. This reduces inventory drastically and increases the return on investments for both main manufacturer and its suppliers.

Just-in-time (JIT) is easy to grasp conceptually i.e. everything happens just-in-time. For e.g.: My journey from home to office on that one lucky day - I left my house and reached the first pick up point to pick my car pool partner just in time. As I arrived on the spot so did he. I reached the toll bridge just in time to pass it without any wait. Then whenever I encountered a traffic signal, it was just in time as I got all of them green. And finally I reached office gate just in time to avoid late entry.

Fish bone: The fishbone diagram identifies many possible causes for an effect or problem. It can be used to structure a brainstorming session. It immediately sorts ideas into useful categories.

The following are three different types of Brainstorming techniques:

- Chit Method: Participants write down their ideas on a piece of paper and hand it over to the person conducting the Brainstorming session.
- Random Technique: Each participant can speak at any time in the group meeting and brainstorming moderator writes down that idea on the board.
- Round robin method: Each participant is given an opportunity to give an idea and that idea is noted on the C&F board.

Fishbone Diagram Procedure:

The fishbone diagram procedure consists of the following steps:

- Agree on a problem statement (effect). Write it at the center right of the flipchart or whiteboard. Draw a box around it and draw a horizontal arrow running to it.
- Brainstorm on the major categories of causes of the problem (in manufacturing setup). If this is difficult use generic headings:
    - Methods
    - Machines (equipment)
    - People (manpower)
    - Materials
    - Measurement
    - Environment
    - Write the categories of causes as branches from the main arrow.
- Brainstorm the major categories of causes of the problem (in Services industry)
    - People
    - Process
    - Procedure
    - Place
    - Environment
- Brainstorm all the possible causes of the problem. Ask: "Why does this happen?" As each idea is given, the facilitator writes it as a branch of the appropriate category. Causes can be written in several places if they relate to several categories.

- Again ask "why does this happen?" about each cause. Write sub–causes branching off the causes. Continue to ask "Why?" and generate deeper levels of causes. Layers of branches indicate causal relationships.
- When the group runs out of ideas, focus attention to places on the chart where ideas are few.

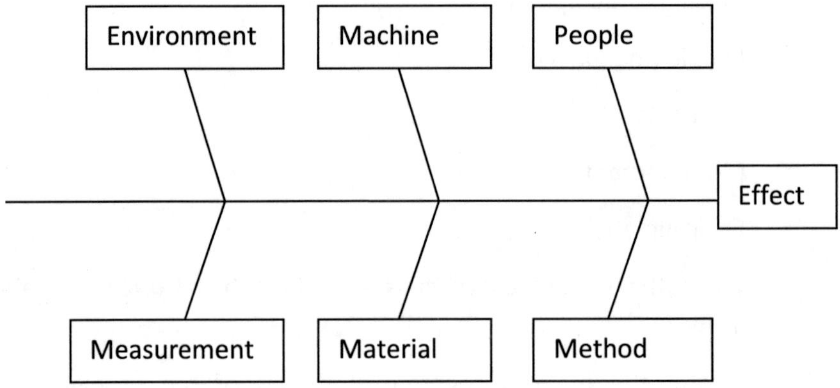

5 Why Analysis:

- 5 Whys is an iterative interrogative technique used to explore the cause-and-effect relationships underlying a problem.
- Not all problems have a single root cause. If one wishes to uncover multiple root causes, the method must be repeated asking a different sequence of questions each time.

Let us see the example to understand it better.

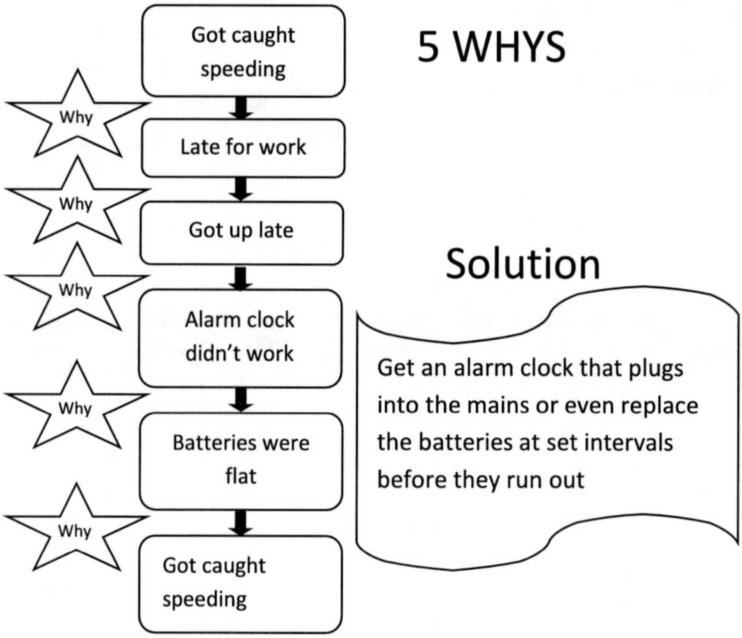

Let us look at another example:

In a web application, a software developer has to create a functionality to upload and download the file and software tester has to test it before the product is finally released to end customer.

After the release, the customer was able to upload the file but was not able to download it. So, 5 why technique was used to identify the root cause and solution:

Example - Software industry

In a web application software tester has to create a functionality to upload and download a file.

Sol 1- Clear requirements should be finalized before the project starts. Both team managers should sign on the requirement documents.

	Failure	Why 1	Why 2	Why 3	Why 4	Why 5
Occurrence	Not able to download the file	Functionality failure	While uploading wrong / non-compliant data entered in the file	No check in the system before upload	Missed while development	Requirements were not clear during development

2nd why actually had 2 answers: one is "No check in the system before upload" (as mentioned above) and the other is "User not aware". So the above chart can be redrawn as per the next figure. This is how we can also deal with multiple root causes by using 5 Why analysis.

Example - Software industry

Sol 2- Prepare and Execute proper training plan before the launch of a new product / software.

	Failure	Why 1	Why 2	Why 3	Why 4	Why 5
Occurrence	Not able to download the file	Functionality failure	While uploading wrong / non-compliant data entered in the file	No check in the system before upload	Missed while development	Requirements were not clear during development
				User Not aware	User Training not done	

5 why analysis should be applied at 2 levels: one is occurrence (which is development stage) and second is detection (testing) stage.

Example - Software industry

Sol - Plan and forecast well for future projects. Try to maximise testing via automation

	Failure	Why 1	Why 2	Why 3	Why 4
Occurrence	Not able to download the file	No proper testing done for this failure mode	Requirements were not clear with the tester	Requirement analysis not done properly	Time constraint and high volume of feature testing

This tool is very effective and can be used in any project to identify the right root cause and solutions.

Heijunka: Before we study Heijunka, we should learn some of the lean terms like, Muda, Muri and Mura:

Muda: Muda is a Japanese word which means 'Waste'. There are two types of wastes - Non-Value-added activities, for e.g.: defects and rework; and Essential Non-Value-added activities, for e.g.: Quality check and Trainings.

Muri: Muri is a Japanese word which means 'Overburden'.

Mura: Mura is a Japanese word which means 'unevenness; irregularity; lack of uniformity; non-uniformity; inequality' and is a key concept in the Toyota Production System. In six sigma terms, it is called variation.

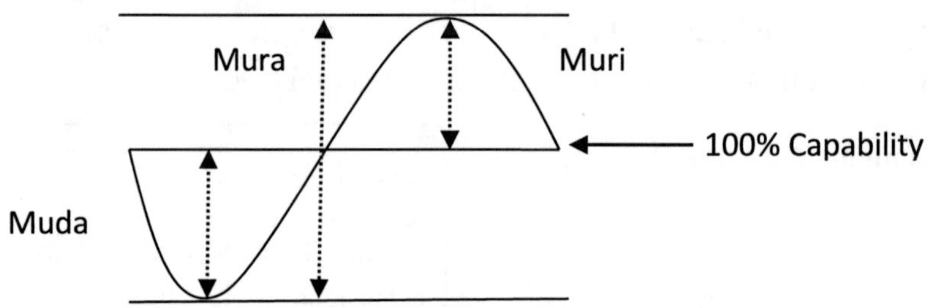

Heijunka:

Heijunka is the foundation of the Toyota Production system and is the process of leveling and sequencing an operation.

There are three main elements of Heijunka:

- Leveling: Overall leveling of a process to reduce variation in output.
- Sequencing: Managing the order in which work is processed (Mixed Production).

- Stability or Standard Work: Reduce process variation.

Let us understand the terms load levelling and sequencing in details.

Load Levelling:

Let's assume there is a 3-step process and the cycle time to process each step is 10 mins, 20 mins and 10 mins respectively. There are 4 people in the process - 2 employees are working at step 1; 1 employee each at step 2 step 3.

It will be as shown in the figure as below:

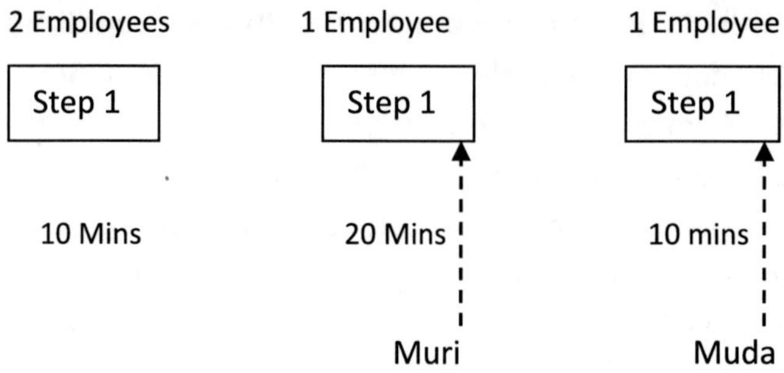

There would be Muri (Overburden) at step 2 as after every 10 mins, 2 products will be produced and pushed to step 2 (it would have extra inventory at step 2) and there would be waiting Muda at step 3 as employee at step 3 will be waiting for 10 mins for next product. This process is not load levelled.

If you level load the process, then the new process will look like as follows. 1 employee at step 1, 2 employees at step 2 and 1 employee at step 3. This rearrangement will reduce the Muda and Muri from the process.

1 Employee	2 Employees	1 Employee
Step 1	Step 1	Step 1
10 Mins	20 Mins	10 mins

Sequencing or mixed production:

Let's say there are 120 reconciliations (50 easy, 30 difficult & 40 most difficult) which have to be finished in 1 month and you have 20 working days. If the work is not sequenced, then 120/20 = 6 reconciliations will be done every day - while performing them, first 8 days (50/6) will be used to finish them which will also include some idle time as these are easy reconciliations; the next 5 days (30/6) would have to worked at 100% productivity as these are difficult reconciliations and last 7 days (40/6) would have to be worked under extreme pressure as these would be the most difficult reconciliations.

This Muda and Muri can be reduced by applying mixed production concept of heijunka like 2 easy, 2 difficult & 2 most difficult reconciliations every day.

Value Stream Mapping:

Value stream mapping is a lean tool that focuses on waste elimination by identifying them through current state map and then reaching to the desired future state through implementation of kaizen improvements. This tool is the heart of the Lean methodology.

The purpose of value stream mapping is to identify and remove or reduce "waste" in value streams, thereby increasing the efficiency of a given value stream. Waste removal is intended to increase productivity by creating leaner operations which in turn make waste and quality problems easier to identify.

- Value stream mapping is a paper and pencil tool that helps you to see and understand the flow of material and information, as a product or service makes its way through the value stream.
- It helps you visualize more than just the single-process level i.e. assembly, welding, etc.
- It helps you to identify not just waste but also the sources of waste in your value stream.
- It provides a common language for talking about manufacturing processes.
- It makes decisions about the flow clearly visible, thereby making it easier to discuss them.
- It ties together lean concepts and techniques and helps you avoid "cherry picking".
- It shows the linkage between the information flow and the material flow.
- It forms the basis of an implementation plan.

There are some basic principles which need to be adhered to:

- Follow the product or services path starting from the customer and then move to the supplier and carefully draw a visual representation of every process.
- Collect basic information to check the velocity of the process at each step.
- Identify wastes.
- Ask a set of key questions and draw a "Future State" map of how value should flow.
- Help us see the sources of waste and eliminate them.

VSM Vs Process Map

S.No	Value stream mapping	Traditional process mapping
1	Customer focused	Functional focused
2	Look at the end to end value stream	Used to understand the steps in a process

Steps to create VSM:

- Step 1 - Identify Customer
  - Customer – Is the individual (s) who are the ultimate beneficiary or the one who consumes/utilizes the output of the process.
  - Identifying customer is a critical cause as lean is based on the fact that you need to look everything from the customers prospective.

We must remember that the supplier feeds you with the inputs and the customer uses the process output.

- Step 2 - Title VSM map with TAKT time & customer

$$\text{TAKT Time} = \frac{\text{(Time) Seconds Available Per Shift (Excluding Overtime)}}{\text{Number of Customer Orders to be Filled Daily}}$$

Total shift time	Lunch break	Tea/Coffee break	Customer demand	TAKT time
9 Hrs	30 Mins	15 Mins	200	148.5 Sec

Total Shift time = 9x60x60=32400 sec

Seconds available per shift = 32400-2700 (30 * 60 + 15 * 60) =29700

TAK Time=29700/200=148.5 sec

- Do not add any stretch time, extra adhoc workers or paid overtime hours in available hours when calculating the TAKT time.
- Customer wants the job to be done in normal hours and does not bother if you have extra individuals working or extra work hours being added for the same.
- If the process timing is 5 PM – 5 AM then the available time would be 12 hrs, but if there is a 24 Hrs support with staggered shifts, the available time would be 24 hrs irrespective of how many agents work in each shift.
- Takt time is only a calculated field and tells you the time in which each unit/product should pass out of the value stream in order to meet the customer expectations.

• Step 3- Lay out process steps

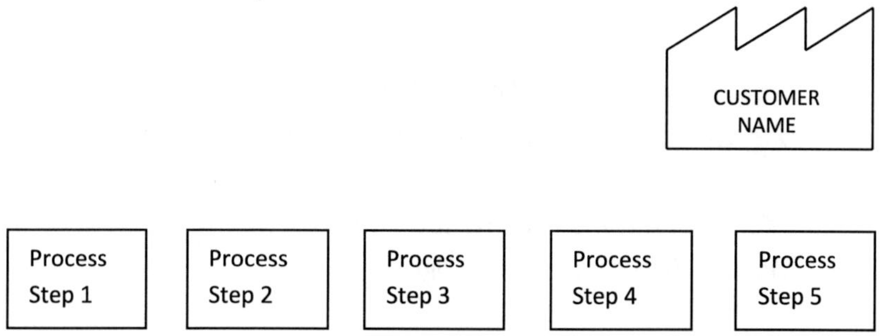

- Just use stickies for each process step and keep pasting them in sequence
- The output step should be on the right and the input step should be on the left.

- Always start from the customer and work your way backward as one should understand customer's perceptive first.
- Anything which happens in continuation without keeping the value in wait is a process element and not a process step.

- Step 4 - Highlight information flow

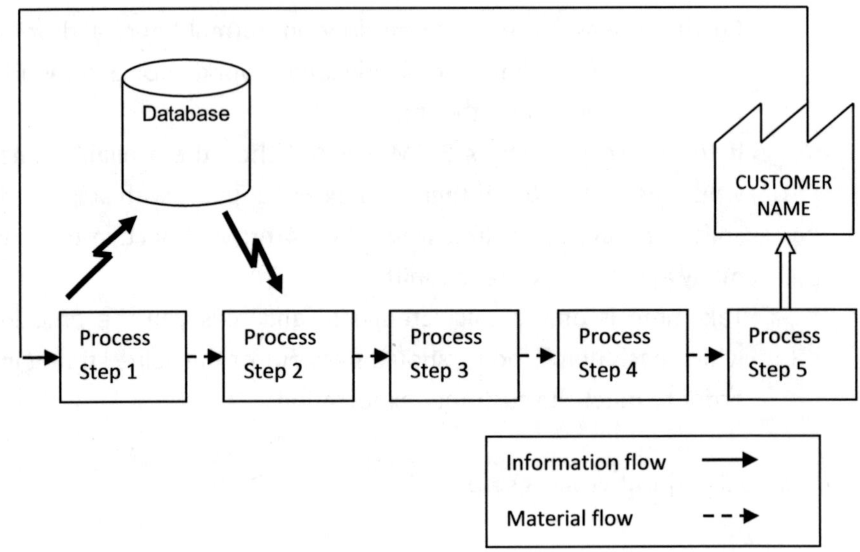

- Create Information & Material Flows on VSM
- Use arrow conventions (e.g., electronic info, manual info, etc.)
- Create IT /data base system Icons
- Information flows from right to left
- Material flows from left to right

- Step 5 - Calculate Rolled first pass yield

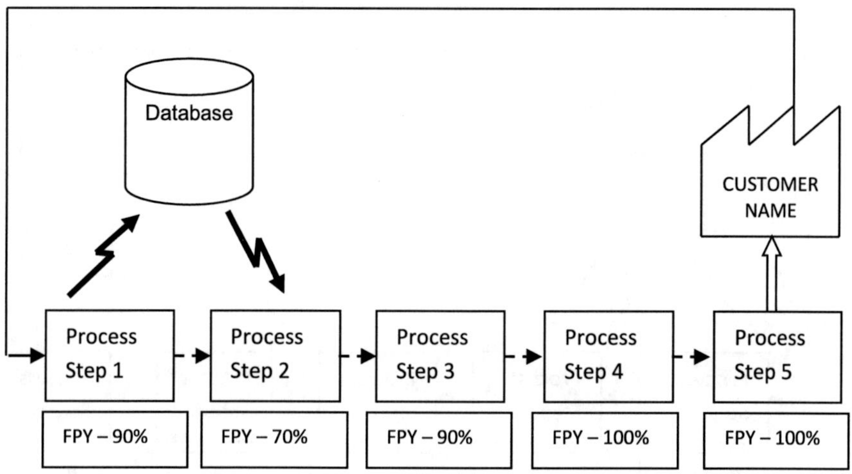

Rolled First pass Yield = FPY step1 X FPY step2 X FPY step3 X FPY step4 X FPY step5

RFPY = 90% X 70% X 90% X 100% X 100% = 56.7%

- If 100 transactions enter step 1 and 5 are errors and 5 transactions need more info from the customer to get processed, then only 90 transactions have cleared step 1 in one go. So, the first pass yield at that step is 90%. Like this one can identify the FPY at all the process steps.
- Rolled first pass yield tells that how many transactions have passed through all the process steps in one go. It is calculated by multiplying FPY of all the process steps. RFPY of 56.7% indicates that only 56.7% of the transactions / products pass through the entire process in one go and rest need rework.

- Step 6 - Create Time Ladder

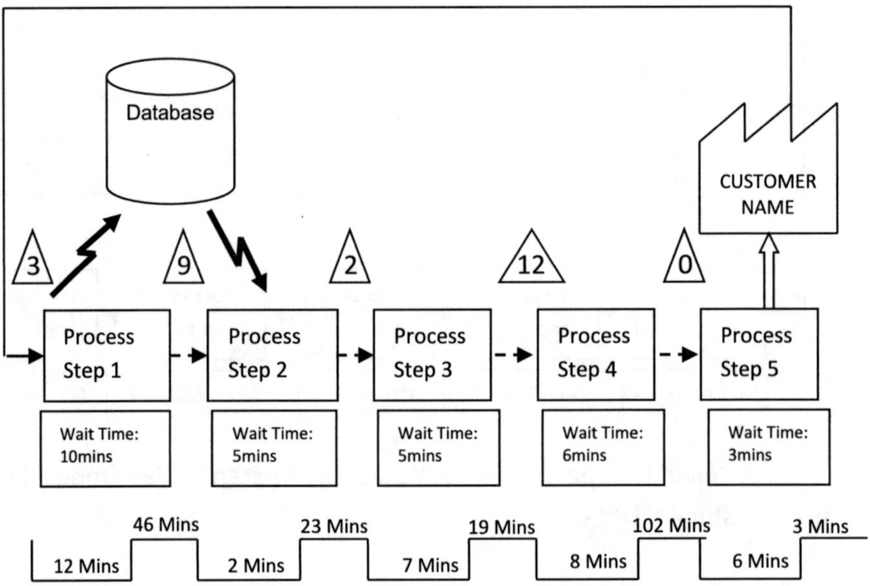

Wait time = Cycle time X Inventory + Observed wait time

Cycle time: The cycle time refers to the time taken by the operators, when they started working on one unit of the product and sent it to the next process step. If you observe that the data collected for cycle time for any process step has huge variation, then you should also capture the SPAN (75th percentile – 25th percentile) to void making decision with skewed data.

Wait Time: This is the **average** time that a unit has to wait before the operator picks it up to start processing in that step. For the first step of the VSM, the wait time is considered from the customer's perspective. For e.g.: if the customer sent a request for credit card at 0900 hrs on Saturday and the operator picked it up on Monday 0900 hrs as he / she does not work on weekends, the wait time would be 48 Hrs and not 0 hrs as the customer has been waiting for it to be processed since Saturday 0900 hrs.

If you find that the data collected for wait time for any process step has huge variation, then you need to also capture the SPAN to avoid making decision with skewed data. (On time ladder wait time is marked in red)

NOTE: The most important thing is to use the same measurement system unit (Mins/Secs/Hrs) for all data capturing to avoid confusion during the end.

Time ladder is nothing but stacking the value add time and non-value-add time for each step, adding it up and then converting it into a ratio which gives the VA/NVA ratio.

VA here would be referred to the cycle time (Assume here that the activities are value add only, if the cycle time is big and has non value add items, then that should have been captured during data collection period as an observation and we then need to use kaizen to reduce the cycle time) and the NVA would be referred to the wait time.

There is a need to understand that there are lots of ways to calculate the NVA and the three most common are listed below. All the three work fine but the most preferred one is the first one as it also takes care of the inventory wait time, which would have not been captured when you were measuring one unit.

1) Observed Wait time + (Inventory * Takt time)

---- Genuinely every unit should be waiting for only a time = Takt time (if you are to complete all units) + wait time of that observed unit.

2) Inventory * Takt time

---- If all the process steps are working to achieve the required speed of production, then every unit including the observed one should wait only for the Takt time.

3) Inventory * Cycle time

---- If the process is already standardized keeping in mind the Takt time, then the Takt time should be same as Cycle time anyways.

Note: All three methods used should give you the same kind of results in the VA/NVA ratio.

- Step 7 Identify Kaizen

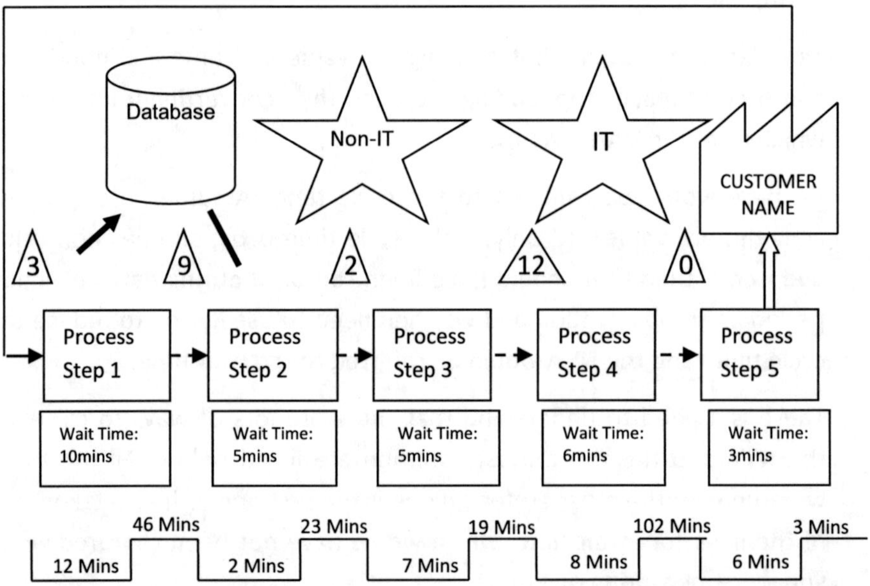

Green color is used to denote the IT kaizens and red color is used to denote the non-IT kaizens

The key is to critique the current state process map that you have mapped and the data that it shows. The more questions you ask about the path your value is taking, the better improvement areas you would come across with.

Try and look at areas like FPY, Information flow (Manual vs. Auto), # of Databases being used, Huge cycle time, Huge inventory buildup, Rework cycles, Huge Wait time along with the observations that you might have captured while data collection on the MUDA in each step to culminate into a list of possible improvement ideas called kaizens.

Kaizen

The term kaizen is a Japanese word adopted into English referring to a philosophy or practices focusing on continuous improvement in manufacturing activities, business activities in general, and even life in general, depending on interpretation and usage.

When used in the business sense and applied to the workplace, kaizen typically refers to activities that continually improve all functions of a business, from manufacturing to management, from quote to cash and any other end to end work stream.

- Step 8: Report out the current state:
- Step 9: Map out the future state map:

Future state VSM is different from the current state VSM in only two ways: -

1) Future state is much clearer as compared to the current state as the current state is an outcome of on-going brainstorming sessions which generally involve a lot of shifting of things from one place to another. On the other hand, the future state VSM is a well-thought out VSM of how you, as a team, want the process to run eventually.

2.) The kaizens listed in the current state and future state differ in the language and objective. Current state VSM kaizens should state the problem (not the solution). While future state VSM kaizen should state the objective (not the problem).

Toyota Production system: When we are learning about Lean and its methodologies, it is also very important to learn about Toyota Production System.

The Toyota Production System empowers team members to optimize quality by constantly improving processes and eliminating unnecessary waste in natural, human and corporate resources. It entrusts employees with well-defined responsibilities in each production step and encourages every team member to strive for overall improvement.

It is also called as lean house of quality

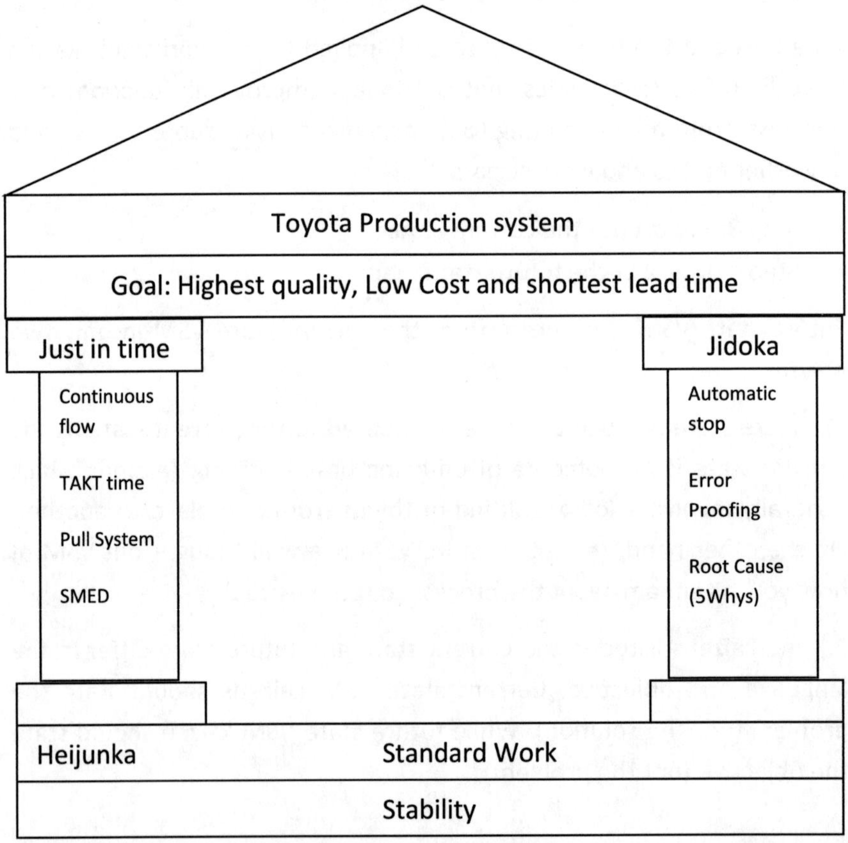

House of Quality

As you can see it looks like a house, so it is called lean house of quality.

The goal of TPS is to produce highest quality at lowest cost with shortest lead time. As the foundation of any house needs to be strong, so the foundation of TPS is strengthen by Heijunka, which is the process of levelling and sequencing an operation. 'Kaizen' means continuous improvement and 'Standard work' means creating the standard procedures to utilize the man power, machine and material in the most effective way.

To form a strong base or culture of quality in any organisations, these three things i.e. Heijunka, Kaizen and Standard work are of utmost importance.

Just in Time and Jidokha form two pillars of TPS. They are very important to first establish the quality culture and then to sustain them for longer period in any organisation.

JIT (Just in time) is achieved through continuous flow which means lining up all steps that truly create value in a rapid sequence or in other words optimizing the flow of information / value across the various steps.

Jidoka's purpose is to free equipment from the necessity of constant human attention and allow workers to staff multiple operations. Jidoka relates closely to Shigeo Shingo's concept of Pokayoke.

Machines that have "human intelligence" built into them have the ability to shut down automatically in the case of an abnormality, in order to stop defective products from flowing into the next process. Jidoka measures are incorporated in the assembly process by use of Andon's and Pin-Pan-Pon - stopping when abnormality is detected.

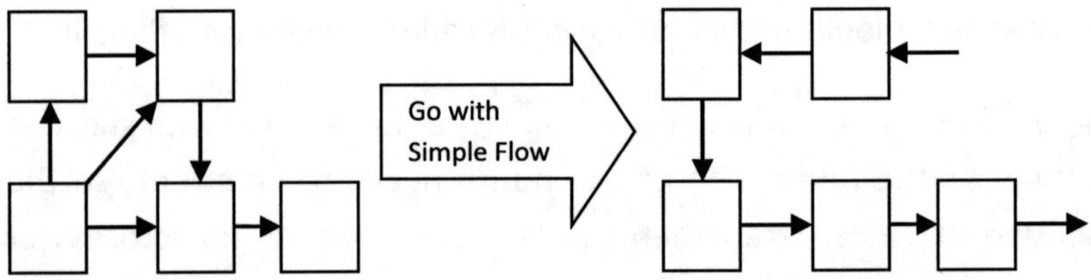

JIT is also supported by Takt time, Pull system and SMED (single minute exchange of die) concepts.

8 steps Lean methodology that can be used to drive continuous improvement projects are:

Step No	Step Description	Tools Used	Deliverable
1	Potential charter & estimate potential business impact	Project charter, CTQ drill down tree, VOC/ VOB chart, ARMI chart	Business case, problem statement, SMART goal, project goal
Project review by Sponsor Champion and Quality leader			
2	Identify process steps, prepare data collection plan, & collect data	DPMO, TAKT time, & Yield Calculations	Data collect & baseline. Collect 30 sample size per subgroup
3	Document current state	Vales Stream Mapping	Current VSM with Lead time ladder
4	Document future state	Value Stream Mapping	Future State Value Stream Map. Lead Time Ladder. Understand Current State to identify all loops and quantify pain areas
Project review by Sponsor Champion and Quality leader			
5	Prioritize Kaizen	Kaizen burst, control impact metrics	List of Kaizen & Kaizen Prioritization
6	Data analysis for the key causes	Box Plot, Pareto, Line Graph, Run Chart, Pie Chart etc.	Identify Key Causes supported with data on Inventory, Cycle Time, Defect Rate / Yield, Volumes, No. Of Operators etc.
7	Action Workout & Implementation	5 Why's & 7 Way's-RCA & Try Storming; 5S, Heijunka, Jidoka, Kanban, Poke Yoke, Andon Boards	Implement key Kaizens & Recommendations; Kaizen News Paper Items, Target Sheets.
8	Pre-Post Metric Comparison, Control Plan & Benefit Realization	Control Charts, Visual Management, FMEA, Mistake Proofing, Communication Plan & Escalation Matrix	Validation of Goal Achievement Sustain Solution & Lessons Learned Documentation. Control Charts, Visual Mngt. Plan implemented on floor, List of issues and calendar for future AWO's created.
Project review by Sponsor Champion and Quality leader			

Let us look at a case study to understand the application of 8 step lean methodology in continuous improvement parlance.

Step 1: Create a project charter.

What is a Project Charter?

A Project Charter is a tool to define the need of a project upfront. It is used to define the focus, scope, direction and motivation for a team. It has six elements:

1. Business Case
2. Problem Statement
3. Goal Statement
4. Project Scope
5. Project Team Charter
6. Milestones - Timeliness to finish the project.

Let us understand each of the elements in detail:

1. **Business Case:** Business Case presents the reason for a particular project. It is a citation written for any project to get management's approval. A good business case should answer the following 3 questions:

   I. What is the (brief) background of the business?
   II. Why should we do this project?
   III. What happens if the project is not done now?

   (1) ***Business background:*** *This is important if you are presenting your charter to someone very senior in the organisation who may not know in detail which part of the business will be impacted by your project. A brief background of the business is helpful in this scenario.*

(a) *For example: ABC bank is a multinational, public sector banking and financial services company dealing with a number of offerings like home and car loans, insurance business and more.*

(2) ***Why and what happens if the project is not done now**: This is also important and needs to be explained to stakeholders- why this project is required and what is the loss to the organisation if this project is not done.*

(b) *For example: As a company, a bank's bad debt in loan books is exceeding the defined targets for the last two years. This is causing the bank cash flow problems and serious recovery strategy problems that is costing them $350 MN every year.*

Now club the two parts and get a perfect business case.

"ABC bank is a multinational, public sector banking and financial services company dealing with a number of offerings like home and car loans, insurance business and more. As a company, the bank's bad debt in loan books is exceeding the defined targets for the last two years. This is causing the bank serious cash flow problem that is costing them $350 MN every year."

c) *Another example of a business case from a manufacturing company could be:*

"XYZ Company is a US-based earthmover company which deals with world-class earth movers and creates a variety of road rollers, bulldozer, crane, and graders. One of their department which deals with cranes is not meeting the final yield target of 97%. Overall, this is causing several rejections, and lower customer satisfaction that is costing the organisation $105 MN per annum and reduction in customer base by 5% every year."

2. **Problem Statement:** This explains the magnitude of the problem. In business case, there could be several issues highlighted; a single problem statement can help define the scope of the project.

   A good problem statement should also include the information *on baseline data.*

   (a) Let's continue with the examples dealt with in business case. Measured over the last six months, bad debt accounts in home loan books have increased by 15%, resulting in a loss of $85 MN.

   (b) Measured over the last six months, the defective rate of products (cranes) from the factory has increased by 20%, resulting in a loss of $10.5 MN for six months cumulative.

3. **Goal Statement:** This defines the expected result from the project in defined timeliness. A Goal Statement should be SMART – Specific, Measurable, Attainable, Relevant and Time bound.

   In the previous two examples, the goal statement will be:

   (a) To reduce the bad debt accounts in home loan books from 25% to 10% by Dec 2016.

   (b) To reduce the defective percentage in cranes from 10% to 3% by Oct 2016.

4. **Project Scope:** Scoping the project is important. Correct scoping can make or break the project.

   Project Scope has two components: In Scope and Out of Scope.

   Scope should also outline the specific details like geography, line of business and functional area.

Taking the previous two examples, the scope would be:

(a) **In Scope:** Bad debts account in the north, east and west regions for home loans only.

Out of Scope: All other bank products and southern region of home loans also.

(b) **In Scope:** Cranes made in Pinang - Malaysia

Out of Scope: Cranes made in other regions like Dallas in the US and Faridabad in India.

5. **Project Team Charter:** For the success of a project, it is important to define / identify a correct team in the beginning. In a Six Sigma project, there are different roles defined as follows:

   (1) **Sponsor:** Is responsible for keeping the project on track towards a successful completion. The sponsor must fulfil several key duties related to the project including launch of the project, signing off on milestones and sponsorship of monetary values if needed for the project. In a customer-driven project, a person with a designation like Sr. Vice President from the customer side could be a sponsor. (It is important to note that the sponsor should be able to approve cost, if needed, for that project).

   (2) **Champion:** Is responsible for the project. The champion is the owner of the project. The project is assigned by the sponsor to the champion and his / her role is to unite the project team and remove roadblocks. His / her other role is to give updates to the sponsor about the project at each phase and ensure honesty within the team.

   (3) **Mentor:** Is a Six Sigma certified resource like Master Black Belt or Black Belt that will help the team with the application of Lean Six Sigma methodologies and tools in the LSS Project.

(4) **Team Members:** Are those who are part of the team and will help the project owner in data collection, brainstorming and then implementing solutions in the later stages of the project.

6. **Milestone:** This defines timeliness for different phases of the LSS project. Below is a template for the same.

   The thumb rule to define the timelines is: assign two weeks to each phase apart from control. Allocate at least two months to control the improved situation.

Start date	End date	Actual end date
Define		
Measure		
Analyse		
Improve		
Control		

What is the importance of the Project Charter?

A project charter is a snapshot of the project. It is an agreement between the management and the project team about what will be delivered though the project in the defined time and scope.

This is a document that formally authorises a project.

Note: In a project charter, 'business case' and 'problem statement' are for the 'management' to review and approve. Goal statement, project scope, milestones and project team charter are for the 'project team'. The goal statement sets the expectation of what the team has to achieve, the scope within which they have to work, the milestones they have to meet, and their roles clearly defined so that each one of them can deliver as per the project's expectation.

Business Case

Background of business
Why should we do this project?
What happens if this project is not done?

Scope

Outline specific details like:

- Geography
- Line of Business
- Functional area

Problem Statement

Quantify the problem (if data is available)
Demonstrate the effect of problem

Milestones

	Start date	End date
Define		
Measure		
Analyse		
Improve		
Control		

Goal Statement

S - Specific
M - Measurable
A - Attainable
R - Relevant
T – Time-bound

Team charter

Champion:
Sponsor:
Mentor:
Process Owner:
Team Members:

Project Charter

Case Study 1 – How to increase email response rate:

- Pine Process is a Back-End Process which replies to Customer Queries (US based). The Process gets 350 email requests daily (average), the process has 5 FTEs with a Turn Around Time of 36 hrs, the process works 6 days a week (9 hours with 2 coffee breaks of 15 min & 1 lunch break of 30 min daily) and usually has a high over time for the L1 team - the avg O/T per day is about 5 hrs (per hour O/T rate is US $5). The team was able to work only on 65% of the emails in the first 36 hours against a target of 95%. The process has been getting low NPS score and is on the verge of a Pull back.
- The first step involves moving mails from the process Inbox (done by 1 FTE) and assigning it to the 2-member L1 team who will research on Oracle. It's been observed that at the start of the day (peak load), the number of mails in the Inbox is about 60. It usually takes about 10 secs to allocate each query to the L1 team.
- The L1 team does the research through Oracle (1min) {the pending queue is about 53}. It takes 1.5 minutes to update info after research into each mail, draft the reply (2 min), which is then sent to the L2 team. Updating & Drafting is done in sequence before sending it to the L2 team, the inventory observed at the Update & Draft process is 7. System Uptime is 92%. (It's been observed that about 75% of the customer emails are sent back for want of basic Information after research.)
- The L2 team consists of 2 FTEs who verify the draft on Oracle Database before forwarding the same to the customer. For about 14% of the cases, a defect is marked for the L1 team & sent back for corrections. The L2 process takes about 45 secs per transactions. The system uptime in this Process step is 94%. The pending queue for L2 is about 4 transactions.
- The number of customer escalations (asking for clarifications) is 1%.

Solution:

Step 1:

a) Create VOC and VOB Chart:

Business – Internal Management | Customer – Pine team

Voice of Business	**Business Issues**	**Critical business requirement**	**Critical customer requirement**	**Customer Issues**	**Voice of Customer**
Customer emails are not answered on time	High Customer dissatisfaction	Respond to customer emails on time	Answer emails on time	Response rate to customers affected Low customer satisfaction	Customer emails are not answered on time

CTQ / CTP – To increase email response rate with in 36 hours from 65% to 95%

b) Create Project Charter:

Business Case	**Scope**
Pine Process is a Back-End Process which replies to Customer Queries (US based). The Process gets 350 E mail (average) requests daily, Team was able to process only 65% of the emails in the first 36 hours against a target of 95%. The Process has been getting low NPS score and is on the verge of a Pull back. This is a 5FTE process and was considered as pilot before transitioning of 500FTE business.	In scope – All invoices Employees reimbursement and vendor invoices. Out of scope – All other processes except invoicing

Problem Statement

Measure over the last 6 months Pine team was not able to meet turnaround time SLA for email process.

Milestones

	Start date	End date
Step 1	15 Jan 18	31 Jan 18
Step 2,3,4	01 Feb 18	03 Mar 18
Step 5,6,7	04 Mar 18	30 Apr 18
Step 8	1 May 18	30 Jul 18

Goal Statement

To improve the email response rate from 65% within 36 hours to 95% by Jul 2018

Team charter

Champion: Process VP
Sponsor: Customer VP
Mentor: Master Black Belt
Process Owner: Pine Process Manager
Team Members: P1 & P2

c) Calculate the potential Business impact:

Before the project is taken for approval to the management, it is important to know the potential impact. Calculation of potential business impact provides the dollar value in terms of loss or gain to the business due to the project and hence strengthens the business case. There are two types of impact - one is tangible and other is non-tangible. Tangible impact is further divided into two types - first is business impact and the second is P&L (Profit and Loss) impact. BI (business impact) impacts the top line of the business and P&L impacts bottom line of the business.

There are different scenarios in a project which can lead to any one of the two types of tangible impacts.

- Increase in revenue and profits – BI and P&L
- Increase in revenue only – BI
- Increase in profits only – P&L Impact
- Increase in cash flow and interest income – BI and P&L
- Loss reduction or cost avoidance leading to increase in profit – P&L

Let us look at some examples to understand the above better:

Example 1: In a leading call centre, the outbound selling team is able to make 1500 successful calls (call where a sale is made) daily.

Base case: Average sale per call is $ 30; cost of operations (Operating cost) is $15 per call; Total revenue generated is 1500X30 = $45,000/-; Total Operating cost is 1500X$15 = $ 22500/-; Total Profit = $45000-$22500 = $22500.

Case 1: Productivity improvement project is done and successful calls per day have gone up to 2000 calls keeping the operating cost same. This would lead to increase in revenue by $ 15000/ - means top line of the business has grown and Overall profit has also gone up by $ 7500 ($30000 - $22500). This is impacting the bottom line of the business.

Business Impact	**Base Case**	**Case I**	**Case II**	**Case III**
Successful calls	1500	2000	1500	1500
Average dollar sales per call	30	30	45	30
Operating Cost	15	15	30	10
Total sales (revenue)	45000	60000	67500	45000
Total Operating Cost	22500	30000	45000	15000
P&L Impact	22500	30000	22500	30000

Case 2: Efficiency of the team has gone up and a sale per call has gone up by $ 15. In this case operating cost has also gone up by $ 15 per call. So the total increase in revenue is $22500 ($67500 - $45000). This will impact the top line of the business. There is only one type of impact in this project.

Case 3: Operating cost per call has been reduced from base case by $5 ($15-$10), with everything else remaining the same. This would increase the overall profit of the business by $7500/-. There would only be one type of impact in this project.

Example 2: A project has been done to reduce the DSO (daily sales outstanding – in how many days company receives the money once the products are delivered) of a company. Before project got initiated, DSO was on 80 days. After the project was done, the DSO was reduced to 75 days. A sale made per day (revenue) is $1,000,000. Total cash flow impact of $ 5,000,000 means $5000000 is received 5 days early and this is leading to an interest generation of $5479.4 {(Principal x Rate x Time /100) (5000000 x .08 x 5/365) rate of interest is 8% (0.08) and time is 5 days divided by 365 days}. This impacts the bottom line of the business, so it is a P&L impact.

Cash Flow Impact	
Present DSO	80 Days
Target DSO	75 Days
Revenue Per day	$1,000,000
Cash flow	$5,000,000
Interest calculated per day	$5479.4
Annualised P&L impact	$2,000,000

Example 3: In the credit card dispute business, bank has to do a charge back to customer in 120 days. If bank misses the deadline then bank cannot charge back customers and they have to write off the amount. This is a loss to the bank. A project has been done to reduce the misses in count of charge back cases (from 1500 to 1000). Amount of chargeback per case is $110 and total loss reduction is $55,000/- (1500 x $110 – 1000 x $110) per month. This is a P&L impact.

Loss Reduction		
Misses in credit card dispute charge backs (count of cases per month)	1500	1000
Amount of chargeback per claim	$110	$110
Amount Lost	$165,000	$110,00
Annualized loss reduction		$660,000

d) ARMI chart & Communication Plan:

ARMI Chart

ARMI stands for Approver, Resource, Member and Interested party.

ARMI chart is a Change management tool which is used to clearly identify roles of each of the project team members during each phase of the project. It helps in clarifying any ambiguity in the roles during the course of the project.

E.g. the following chart clearly outlines the roles of each concerned party:

	Different Phases of methodologies				
DMAIC	Define	Measure	Analyse	Improve	Control
8 Step Lean	Step 1	Step 3	Step 5	Step7	Step 8
Project Sponsor	A	I	A	I	A
Project Champion	A	A	A	A	A
Six Sigma MBB	A	A	A	A	A
Business Leader	I	I	I	I	I
Black Belt	R	R	R	R	R
Subject Matter expert	M	M	M	R	R
Trainer	M	M	M	R	M

A represents the approver - These are stakeholders who need to approve a phase of the project.

I represent interested party - These are stakeholders who do not have to approve in that phase. They are only interested in the output delivered during that phase of the project.

R is the resource - These are the stakeholders whose niche skills are required during the project. For example - black belt is a resource as he / she brings in six sigma tools and methodology skills. If somebody from

IT department is needed to develop a macro in improve phase will become a resource in that phase.

M represents member of a project who is part of the project and can help in various project related activities like brainstorming, data collection, value stream mapping and solution identification etc.

Communication plan

It is also important to communicate the work done to the stakeholders at different stages of any project, hence a communication plan should be made and circulated in the beginning of the project.

Effectiveness of the communication plan will only be felt if it is executed properly. A plan only on paper is no plan. Following template can be used for a communication plan:

Event	**Message**	**Audience**	**Frequency**	**Responsibility**	**Medium**
Project Team meeting	Project progress update	Project team	Once/ week	Project owner	Face to face meeting
Stakeholder review	Project update	All-important stakeholders	End of each phase	Project owner	Conferenc e call
Project update	Progress made & next steps	All stakeholders	Bi weekly	Project owner	Email

Step 2: Prepare data collection plan

Define measures		Operational definition		Data collection		
What is to be measured	Data type	Definition	Formula used	Where	When	How
Email response rate	Binary discrete	No of emails responded daily	Total emails responded/ Total emails received	In Excel template	15 Apr	Collect data from day end system report
Cycle time data at each step	Continuous	Time taken to process each step	No formula	On the floor	20 Apr	Sit with the processor and record live
Calculate FPY at each process step	Discrete	Total work without rework	Total correct output without rework / total input	In excel template	20 Apr	Do a sample base audit and upload information

Step 3: Create Current State Value Stream Map for the defined case and identify the TAKT time

The process gets around 350 email requests daily. A regular day consists of 9 hours with 2 coffee breaks of 15 min each & 1 lunch break of 30 min

Takt time = Available time / Total customer demand

Available time = (9x60x60 = 32400 sec) – (60*60) = 28800 Sec

Total customer demand = 350 emails

Takt time = 28800/350 = 82.28 Sec

It means after every 82.28 Sec an email should be processed otherwise process will not be able to match customer demand.

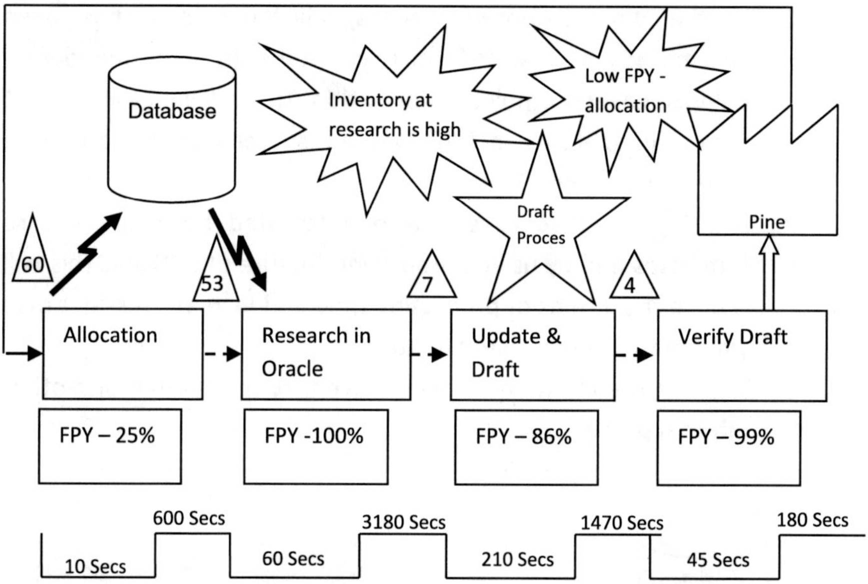

Total value-added time = 325 Sec

Total non-value-added time = 5430 Sec

Process efficiency = 325 / (325+5430) = 5.6%

Rolled First Pass Yield (RFPY) = FPY1 x FPY2 x FPY3 x FPY4

= 25% x 100% x 86% x 99%

= 21.3 %

This means only 21.3% of the total emails worked in the process go without rework.

Step 4:

Now define the future state process map in which the new process needs to be followed:

1. In the new proposed process, allocation step has been automated and a web form is created with some mandatory fields to collect complete information. This will increase the first pass yield at step 1 to 100% and a resource would also be free to work on other initiatives.
2. Drafting the responses is also automated through standard templates and by using automation feature of outlook. This will reduce the 2 mins of processing time and increase the first pass yield of that process step to 100%.
3. Training the team on errors received from customer and other internal process audits.

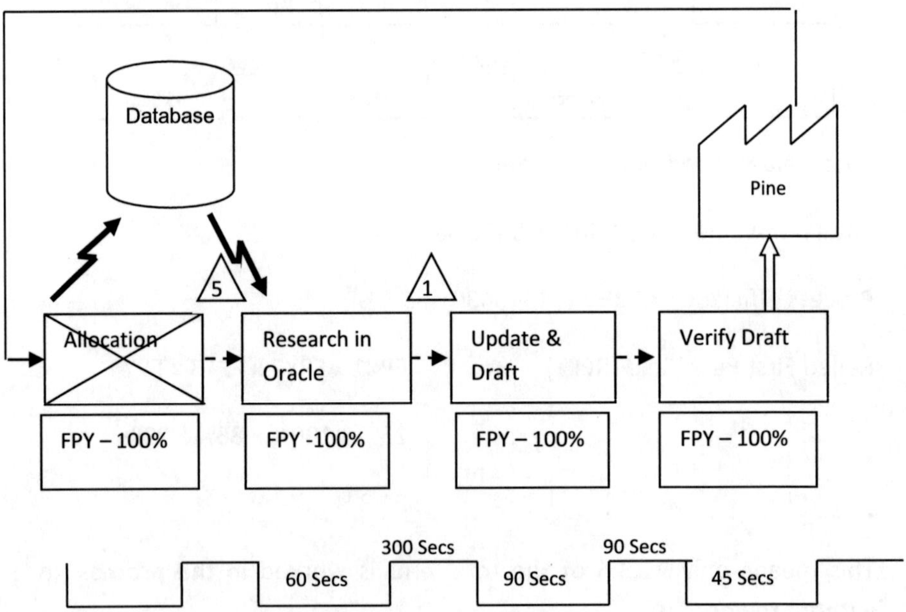

Future State Value Stream Map

After the Future state the process efficiency would go up:

Total value-added time = 195 Sec

Total non-value-added time = 390 Sec

Process efficiency = 195/ (390+195) = 33%

Rolled First Pass Yield (RFPY)	=	FPY1 x FPY2 x FPY3 x FPY4
	=	100% x 100% x 100% x 100%
	=	100 %

In the new process there is no rework as RFPY of the process is 100%.

Step 5: Kaizen Prioritization: Tools that can be used to prioritize the kaizens could be Ease Impact metric or Ease Impact diagram. So, Ease Impact diagram is subjective and Ease impact metric would be objective and some numbers can be used to prioritize kaizens.

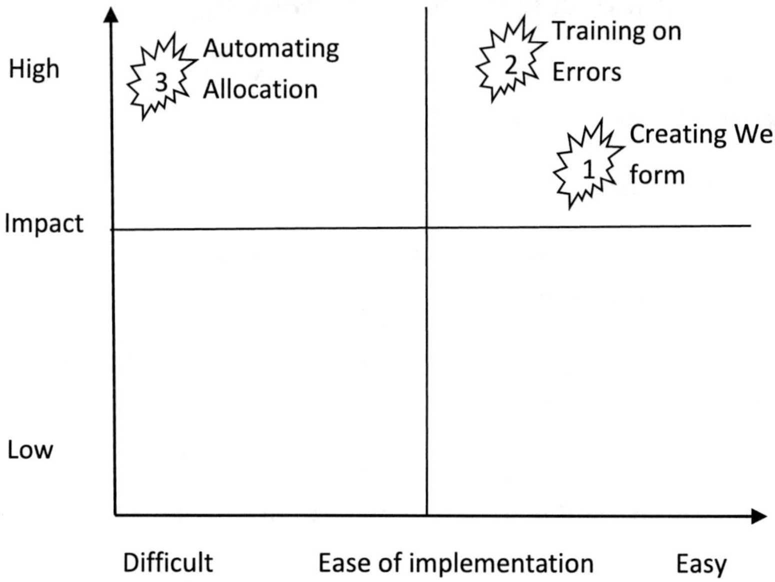

Ease Impact Diagram

Ease Impact diagram is used first where it is easy to implement and has higher impact. So from the list of given kaizens, creating web forms, training on errors and automation were picked up as they were easy to implement and have higher impact.

Same thing can be achieved with ease and impact metrics. In this tool other factors can also be included like: Cost of implementation.

S. no	Kaizen	Ease	Cost	Impact	Total E*C*I	Rank of Implementation
1	Creating web form	4	4	5	80	1st
2	Training on errors	5	4	3	60	2nd
3	Automating allocation	3	3	3	27	3rd

Prioritizing the Solution Kaizens

After you prioritize the kaizens, you can start the data analysis and then start implementing them accordingly

Step 6: Data analysis

Kaizen 1: In this case, data analysis was done to identify top contributing errors and that helped in creating a training plan.

Pareto chart and pareto principle were used to prioritize top 80% of the contributors.

The Pareto Principle (80/20 rule): The Pareto principle states that, for many events, roughly 80% of the effects come from 20% of the causes.

Use of Pareto: During any project, the intention of the project lead is to identify and work on those minimum causes which can have maximum impact the project goal. Pareto chart helps quality professionals to identify those top 20% causes.

S.No	Error Type	Count
1	Salutation Errors	98
2	Spelling Errors	87
3	Incorrect Name	77
4	Incorrect Readings	60
5	Punctuation Errors	24
6	Grammatical Errors	19
7	Incorrect Address	12
8	Incorrect Account	11
9	Incorrect Amount	9
10	Duplicate letters	7

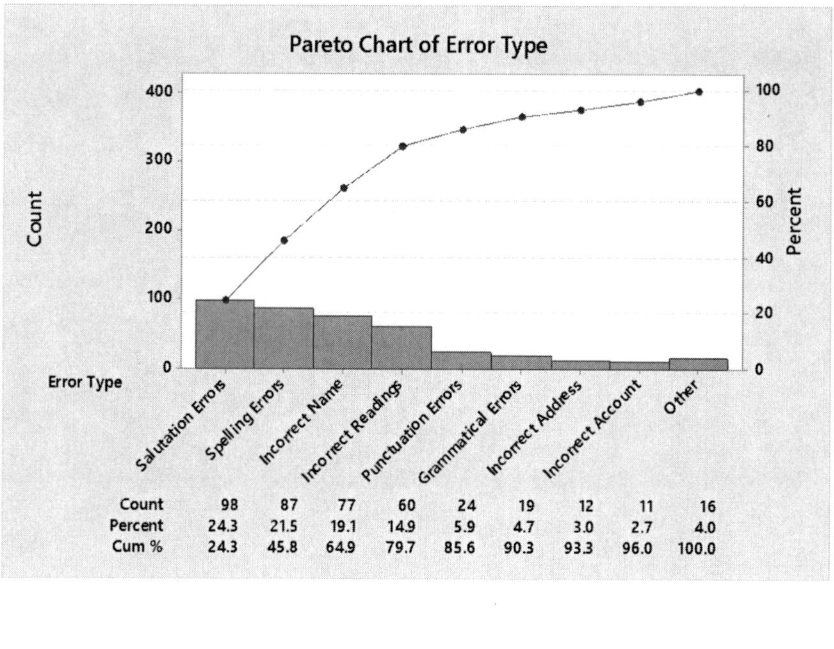

So, the top 79.7% contributors are Salutation errors, Spelling errors, Incorrect names and Incorrect readings. Now the trainer is not required to train on all error types, however trainer can make training plan on these 4 error types and improvement in them will improve the overall process.

Kaizen 2: Second big kaizen was on creating web form that would help the team to gather the complete and accurate information in the first go. '5S' was used to eliminate all unnecessary columns from the printed form and then it was digitized as a web form.

Customer Form

1 .First Name	
2. Middle Name	
3. Last Name	
4. Customer Address	
5. Email Address	
6. Account No	
7. Marital Status	
8. Permanent Address ✕	
9. Mobile No	
10. Product Description	
11. Contact details ✕	
12. Employed ✕	

After removing all the unnecessary columns, the webform was designed.

Kaizen 3: After automated (Jidhoka) allocation of work, some internal logics were built to automatically assign the equal distribution of emails to all resources.

Step 7: Action workout

Next step is to create action workout on the kaizens and the tool that can be used is '4W1H'

4W1H: What/When/Where/Who and How

What is to be implemented	When it is to be implemented	Where to be implemented	Who will implement	How to implement
Create web form	15 Dec 20**	In HTML	IT team manager	Create a webform by using the current available check list
Training plan on error types	20 Dec 20**	In Tiger meeting room	Training manager& Quality manager	Use pareto to identify top contributing errors and create training plan on them
Automate email allocation	24 Dec 20**	In Outlook	IT team manager	Build a logic to create the automatic email allocation to the employees

This tool will help create an action plan for all the actionable solutions.

It is important to identify failure modes of the newly-identified solutions before they are implemented in the process. The tool that can be used for this is 'FMEA'.

FMEA stands for Failure Mode and Effect Analysis
Failure modes are any errors or defects in a process, design or item, especially those that affect the customer - they can be potential or actual.

Effect Analysis refers to studying the consequences of those failures.

Solution Step	Potential Failure Mode	Severity	Occurrence	Detection	RPN	Mitigates
Auto data collection	Webpage Crash	8	5	5	200	Auto trigger to IT SPOC if webpage crashes
	Webpage slow	6	7	4	168	Create a separate frequency band

There is a predefined scale on which severity, occurrence and detection has to be rated.
If the failure mode is very severe, like it can cause injury or death to an employee or customer, then it should be rated 10.
Severity: Missing a service level agreement for a BPO could be severe enough to be rated 9.

Occurrence: This means how many times the SLA got missed due to this new idea getting implemented, so chances are less as people are tenured enough. It has a similar cycle time to process the transaction, hence a lower score of 2 is given.

Detection: This has to be inversely proportional, which means the more you are able to detect the defect before it occurs, the lesser the score. In the above example, there is a tool to track and identify the SLA misses, hence a lesser score is given on detection.

RPN: RPN is the product of 'S', 'O' and 'D' i.e. 'S' x 'O' x 'D'. If this number is greater than 100, then mitigation is to be applied before the solution is finally implemented in the process. If this number is less than 100, then the solution can be implemented immediately.

Step 8: Create Pre and Post comparison and create control plan

Pre and post comparison: Show value-added and non-value-added time reduction before and after the project. Validate the findings with hypothesis tests.

Check your data if it is continuously normal or non-normal and choose the test accordingly. For the present project, data is continuous and normal and so one-way 'annova' test is done. ('Annova' test is a type of hypothesis testing. For further updates on hypothesis testing refer to my book '8 steps to problem solving'. You can also visit my youtube channel by the name of 'Six Sigma by MBB Mohit Sharma')

For this analysis 30 data points were considered before and after the project.

Before Project		After Project	
Cycle Time	Wait Time	Cycle Time	Wait time
322.390	5430.65	193.523	390.326
325.432	5428.36	193.453	390.454
326.430	5432.21	195.042	390.797
327.605	5434.13	195.804	389.896

325.887	5427.90	194.354	389.895
327.778	5431.39	193.525	390.334
329.025	5430.27	195.687	389.334
321.977	5430.67	193.300	389.974
327.202	5425.14	195.613	389.860
326.857	5430.97	195.807	391.602
325.952	5430.11	194.840	388.232
324.273	5426.90	193.886	390.448
325.087	5429.87	193.260	390.486
324.115	5430.72	194.610	389.131
325.632	5425.03	195.886	390.057
327.124	5426.89	196.313	390.145
325.812	5428.55	195.842	389.710
329.062	5433.43	195.028	389.257
326.344	5424.71	195.200	390.603
325.486	5425.79	195.552	389.371
323.192	5426.41	193.876	388.831
326.810	5432.04	194.533	391.471
324.443	5427.24	195.442	390.607
322.582	5429.58	196.644	388.184

324.885	5432.55	195.293	389.465
328.781	5431.25	194.590	390.524
325.315	5429.75	194.863	391.937
325.510	5432.73	194.411	390.689
325.637	5431.92	193.476	389.119
325.962	5427.21	195.177	389.069

One-way ANOVA: Before Project cycle time, After Project Cycle time

Method

Null hypothesis: All means are equal
Alternative hypothesis: At least one mean is different
Significance level: $\alpha = 0.05$

Equal variances were assumed for the analysis.

Factor Information

Factor	Levels	Values
Factor	2	Before Project cycle time, After Project Cycle time

Analysis of Variance

Source	DF	Adj SS	Adj MS	F-Value	P-Value
Factor	1	257121	257121	121565.31	0.000
Error	58	123	2		
Total	59	257244			

Since P value is less than 0.05, there is statistically significant difference between before and after project cycle times.

One-way ANOVA: Before Project wait time, after project wait time

Method

Null hypothesis: All means are equal
Alternative hypothesis: At least one mean is different
Significance level: α = 0.05

Equal variances were assumed for the analysis.

Factor Information

Factor	Levels	Values
Factor	2	Before Project wait time, After project wait time

Analysis of Variance

Source	DF	Adj SS	Adj MS	F-Value	P-Value
Factor	1	380946286	380946286	96958198.94	0.000
Error	58	228	4		
Total	59	380946514			

Since P value is less than 0.05 hence there is statistically significant difference between before and after project wait times.

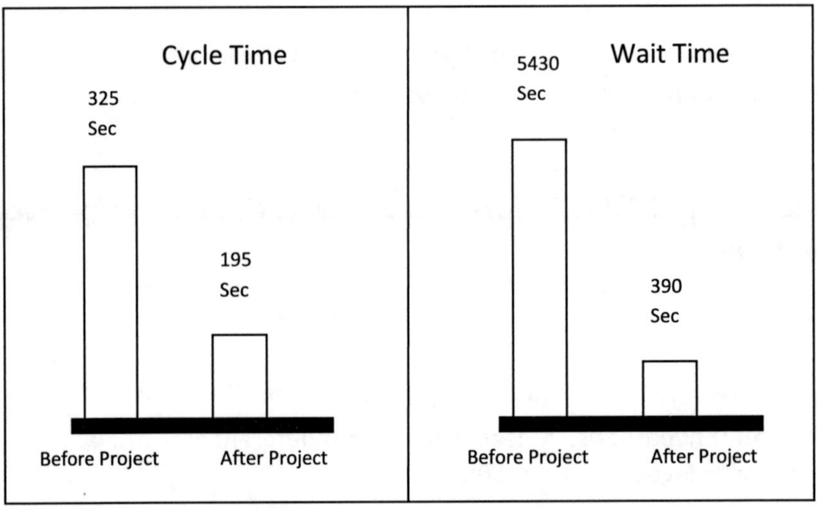

Next step is to create a control plan.

A control plan is a method of documenting the significant functional elements of improved process to control them which in turn will keep the improved process under statistical control. A control chart can be made in different ways, let us learn the most simple and effective way.

What	When	Where	Who	How	Frequency of check	Checked by
Monitor 10% processed emails	Every day	Store data in shared drive	Quality Check resource	Pick up sample by using stratified random sampling	Weekly monitor the QC resource and QC data	Quality Manager and Process Manager

Using the above all the things which will control the improved state of the process can be put as part of control plan and can be tracked.

Next step is to create a control chart and see if the process is in statistical control or not.

Control Chart:

- The control chart is a graph used to study how a process changes over time.
- A control chart always has a central line for the average, an upper line for the upper control limit and a lower line for the lower control limit. So, we can call it a time series plot with control limits.
- The control limits are +-3 standard deviation from the center line.

For continuous Data

Sample is subgroups average with subgroup sizes (Subgroup size >8)	X bar & Standard deviation chart (X bas - S chart)
Sample is subgroups average with subgroup sizes (Subgroup size 2~8)	X bar & Range chart (X bas - R chart)
Sample is individual measurements (Subgroup size 1)	Individual and moving range chart (IMR)

For Discrete data

	Defects	Defectives
Constant Lot Size	C	NP
Variable Lot Size	U	P

- As the data is continuous and it has 1 sample size per subgroup, so IMR chart is used.

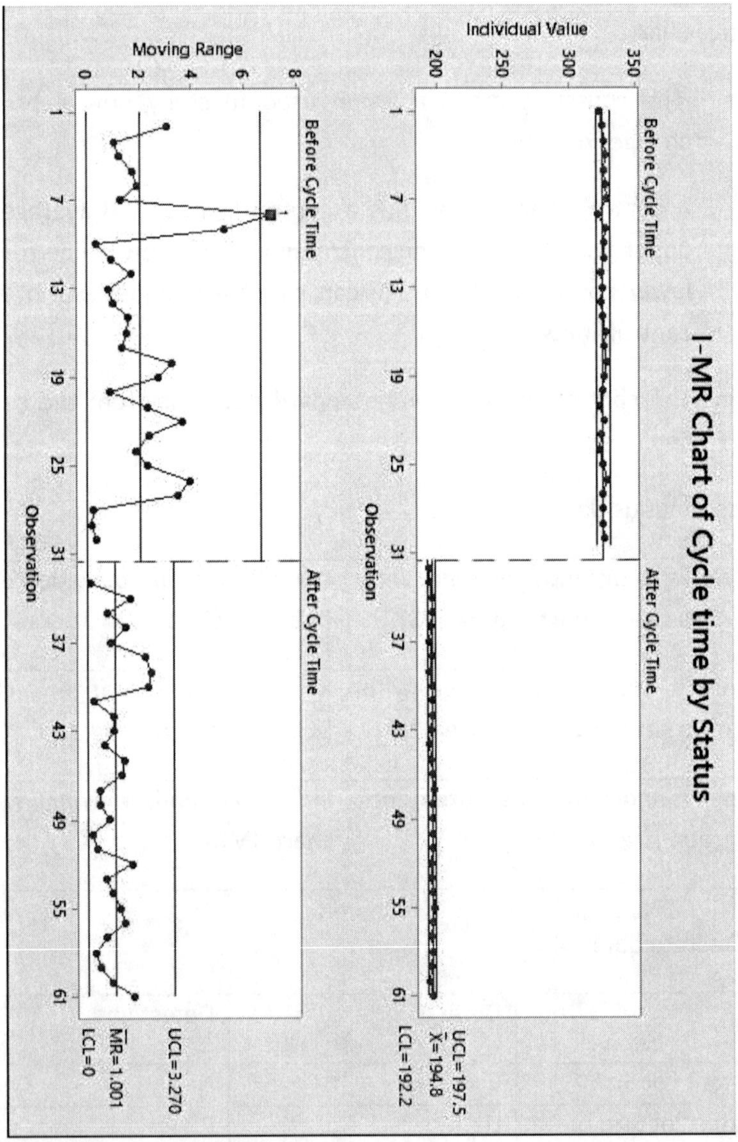

In I chart the average of 325 Mins has been reduced to 194.8 Mins and Range chart shows the reduction in variation of the data also.

Case Study 2 – Reduce turnaround time of invoice processing in Finance and accounting process

For an MNC in India, all employee services and F&A claims come through the mailroom process. This process had 19 people (9 Skilled, 9 Semi Skilled and one team leader) to render these services. There was a huge backlog to the tune of 2000 cases. Some of the teams in the mailroom were consistently working for 10+ hours. There were strong follow-ups from suppliers and staff due to delay in mailroom processing and team was losing the physical invoices.

The team was able to process only 49% of the invoices within 3 working days and a target of processing 98% of the invoices within 3 working days was given to continuous improvement team.

Data verification and entry takes 0.75 mins to process an invoice and there was an observed wait time of 640 minutes before the work begins. There are total 5 FTEes working in this team.

SAP inward process takes 0.33 Minutes and an observed wait time of 41.6 Minutes. The process has an inventory of 130 invoices and it's a 5 FTEs' process.

Next process is scanning the invoices and it takes 0.33minutes to scan an invoice. There is an observed wait time of 3.2 minutes before this process. This is a 3 FTEs' process with average inventory of 10 invoices.

After the Scanning Process, Indexing is done and it takes 0.33 minutes to index the invoice. There is an observed wait time of 9.6 minutes and average inventory of 30 invoices.

The last step is dispatch and it takes 0.33 minutes to dispatch the invoice with an observed wait time of 0.32 minutes. Average inventory is 1 at this step and it is 2 FTEs' process.

Solution:

Step 1: a) Create VOC and VOB Chart

Business – Internal Management | Customer – Company Employees / Vendors

Voice of Business	Business Issues	Critical business requirement	Critical customer requirement	Customer Issues	Voice of Customer
Invoices are not processed correctly and not in time	High Employee and Vendor dissatisfaction	Process all invoices correctly and within TAT	Process all invoices correctly and within TAT	Delay in payment Incorrect payment	Invoices are processed on time Invoices are lost

CTQ / CTP – To increase the invoice processing from 49% within 3 days to 98% in 3 days.

b) Next step is to create a Project Charter

Business Case	Scope
Acorn is a mailroom process for an MNC in India. In this Organisation all employee services and F&A claims comes through the mailroom process. This is a 19 FTE process which has a broken process and has a backlog of 2000 cases. The processing of the invoices within 3 working days was only 49%, most of the teams were working more than 10 hours a day. The team was loosing some of the important invoices and had some compliance issues as well	In scope - US email process Out of scope – All other processes related to Pine account

Problem Statement	Milestones		
Measure over the last 6 months team was able to process only 49% of the invoices within 3 working days and a target of processing 98%		**Start date**	**End date**
	Step 1	**15 Apr 18**	**30 Apr 18**
	Step 2,3,4	**01 May 18**	**30 May 18**
	Step 5,6,7	**01 Jun 18**	**31 Jul 18**
	Step 8	**01 Aug 18**	**30 Sep 18**
Goal Statement	**Team charter**		
To increase the invoice processing from 49% within 3 days to 98% in 3 days by Sep 2108.	Champion: Process VP Sponsor: Customer VP Mentor: Master Black Belt Process Owner: Acorn Process Manager Team Members: A1, A2 & A3		

Step 2: Data collection plan

Define measures		Operational definition		Data collection		
What is to be measured	Data type	Definition	Formula used	Where	When	How
Cycle time and wait time at each step of the value chain	Continuous	Cycle time – Time taken to perform a step Wait time – Time between two steps	Cycle time: Finish time – start time Wait time: Start time of next step – finish time of previous step	In Excel template	07 May	Take sample and collect data by physically recording time with the help of stop watch
Calculate FPY at each process step	Discrete	Total work without rework	Total correct output without rework / total input	In excel template	10 May	Do a sample base audit and upload information

Step 3: Current State Value Stream Map

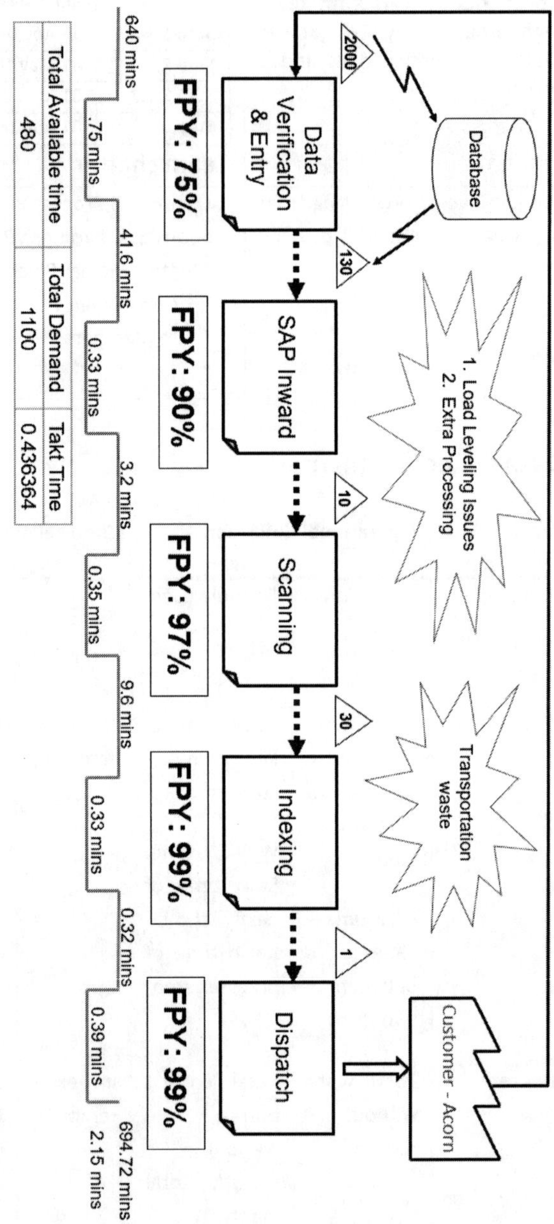

Step 4: Future State Value Stream Map

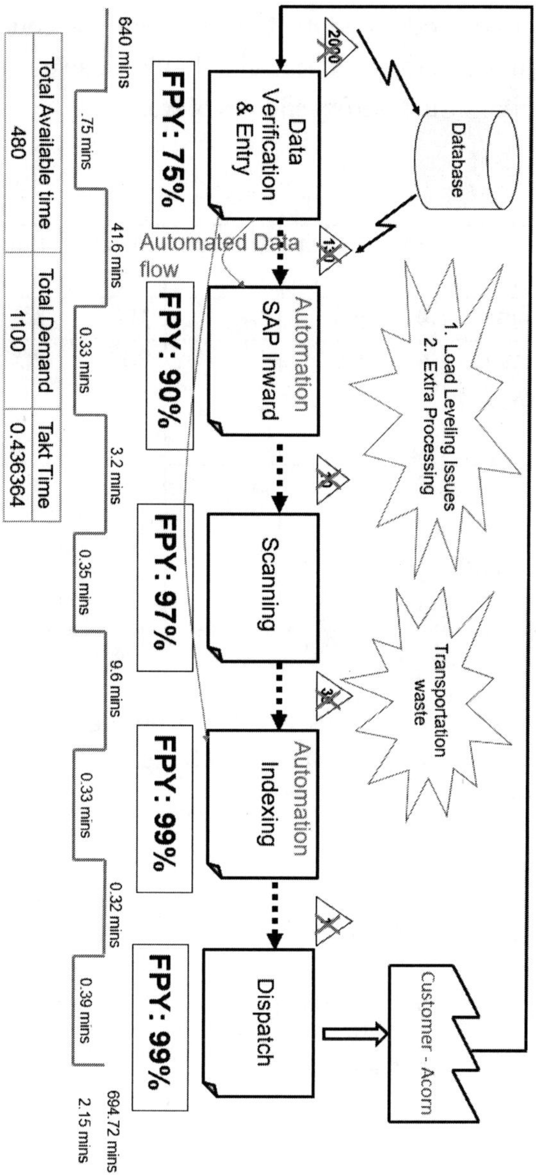

Step 5: Data analysis and root cause identification:

All lean VSM projects should not just limit themselves to identifying waste but also to extend the scope to understand the sources of those wastes. Through their project, black belts should be able to identify root causes and solutions for different sources of wastes

S. no	Kaizen	Ease	Cost	Impact	Total E*C*I	Rank of Implementation
1	Cross training	4	5	5	100	1st
2	Implementation of automated tools	4	4	5	80	2nd
3	Change mailroom location and layout	3	3	5	45	3rd

Ease-Impact Score is a Product of Score given to Ease of Implementation, Cost of the idea (should be less for more score) & to Impact of Action.

Scale: Ease 1-5, 5=Easiest

cost 1-5, 5=Costliest

Impact 1-5, 5 =Highest

Step 6: Identifying solutions with data analysis:

Solution 1:

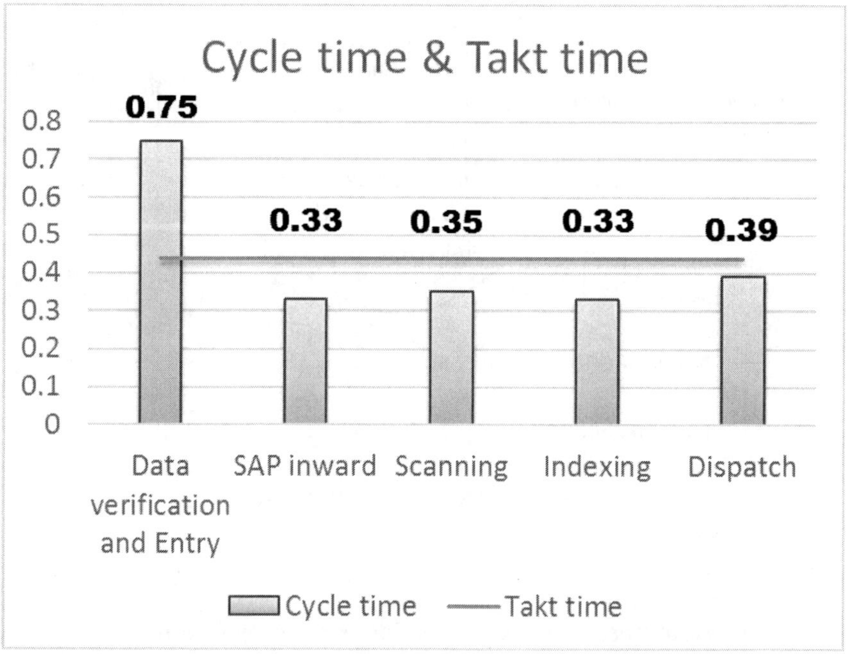

Heijunka Load Leveling issue

- Cross Training of skilled and semi-skilled resources, so that they could be utilized as per daily needs.
- Work allocation and job allocation daily as per availability of resources.
- Use of automated systems rather than manual efforts

Extra Processing Solution 2:

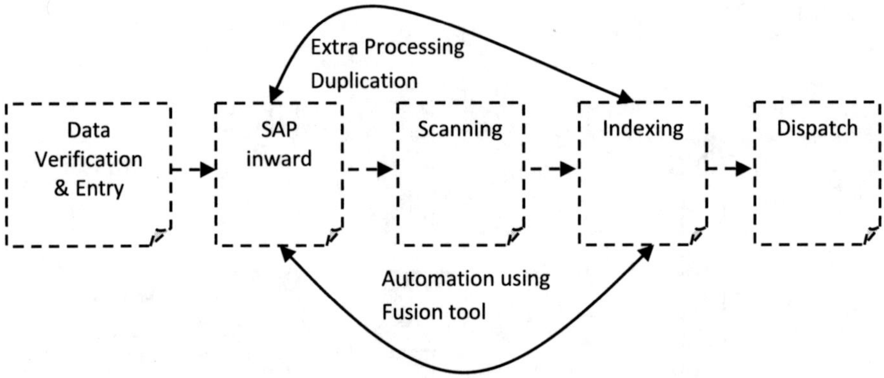

- No data entry in entry stage
- Upfront Scanning
- Removal of SQL macro-based workflow
- Move data entry to SAP
- Automate SAP inward and indexing using fusion

Solution 3:

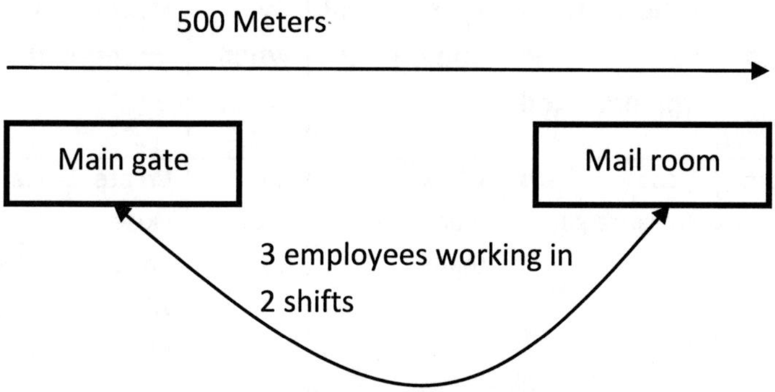

The mail room was shifted close to the main gate, where courier guys would deliver the mail directly and hence loss/delay of invoices received were eliminated.

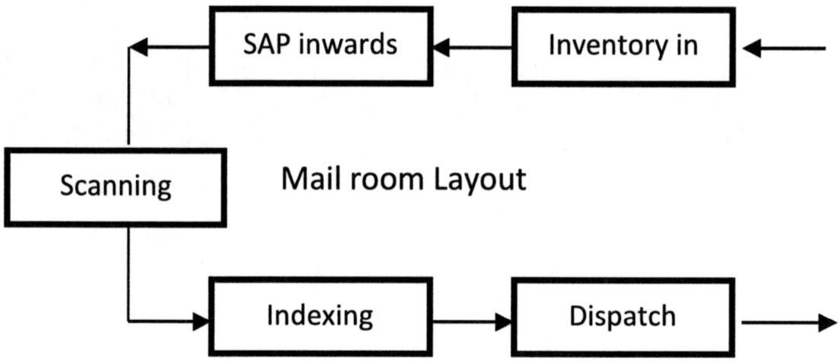

Change in the layout of the department, with teams sitting in a semicircle—team members could turn around and talk to each other.

Step 7: Implementation plan:

What is to be implemented	Where it is to be implemented	Who will implement	By when	How it is to be implemented
Shift mail room	Close to entrance gate	Work place management team	20 May 18	Create an area close to entrance with sitting capacity of 20 employees
Cross Training	In Atlas Meeting room	Training manger	25 May 18	Create training and ramp up plan
Implementation of automated tools	In the mail workflow	IT manager	9 Jun 18	Implement the tool and check all the failure modes before go live

Step 8: Pre and Post project improvements

Before and after project status:

	Dec **	Jan**	Feb**	Mar**	Lean Project Initiation	Jun**	Jul**	Aug**	Sep**
Total Processed	26825	37050	28092	34805		26812	27815	28732	26854
Processed within in 3 days	13134	24508	17158	19852		26468	27758	28658	26796
Processed after 3 days	13691	12542	10934	14953		344	57	74	58
DPU	0.510382	0.338516	0.389221	0.429622		0.01283	0.002049	0.002576	0.00216
Process Sigma	1.473973	1.916518	1.78135	1.677336		3.731317	4.370479	4.297433	4.353823

Control Chart:

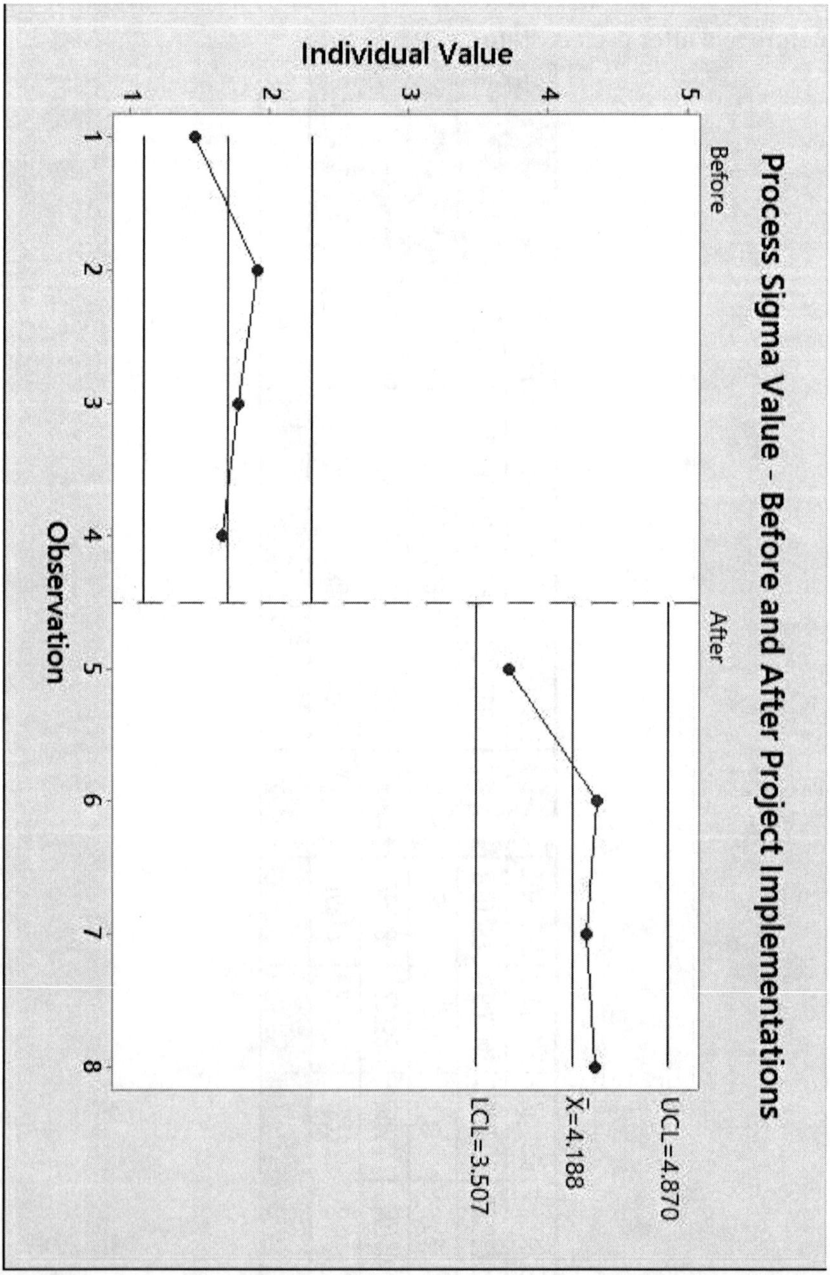

Case Study 3: Reduce software development turnaround time

A UK based multinational makes pen drives along with its drivers (Drivers are the software which help the instruments talk to the other devices. Like if you insert Pen drive in your laptop, the first step is that a driver (software) is installed to access the Pen drive).

The problem was that the company was able to deliver only 14% of the drivers on time. So, the team took this as a lean project to improve the on-time delivery from 14% to 70%.

Step 1:

a) Understand the Voice of the Customer and Voice of the Business

Business – Internal Management			Customer – Internal Manufacturing Division		
Voice of Business	**Business Issues**	**Critical business requirement**	**Critical customer requirement**	**Customer Issues**	**Voice of Customer**
Delay in driver developm ent leading to delay in Pen-drive delivery	Delay in Pen-drives is leading to loss of customer base	Deliver Pen-drives on time	To receive the Drivers on time as agreed	Delay in receiving the drivers delays overall shipment	Drivers to the Pen-drives are not delivered on time

CTQ / CTP – To increase on time delivery from 14% to 70% in phase I by Dec **

b) Create Project Charter

Business Case

ABC Company manufactures Pen-drives. One of the leading manufacturers.

Drivers are the software which help the instruments talk to the other devices. Like if you insert Pen drive in your laptop, the first step is that a driver(software) is installed to access the Pen drive. So, this organization was manufacturing Pen-drive and their driver.

The problem was that the company was able to deliver only 14% of the drivers on time. This was leading to delay in the overall product delivery and un happy customers.

Scope

In Scope: Pen-drive Drivers

Out of Scope: any other division

Problem Statement

Measured over the last 6 months the on-time delivery of drivers is only 14% as against a target of 70% & impacts the customer's satisfaction score.

Milestones

	Start date	End date
Step 1	**15 Jun** **	**13 Aug** **
Step 2,3,4	**14 Aug** **	**15 Oct** **
Step 5,6,7	**16 Oct** **	**30 Nov** **
Step 8	**01 Dec** **	**31 Dec** **

Goal Statement

To improve the overall on-time delivery for the drivers developed by the team from 14% by 70% by Dec **

Team charter

Champion: Process VP
Sponsor: Customer VP
Mentor: Master Black Belt
Process Owner: ABC Team Manager
Team Members: ABC1, ABC2 & ABC3

c) Create High Level Process Map

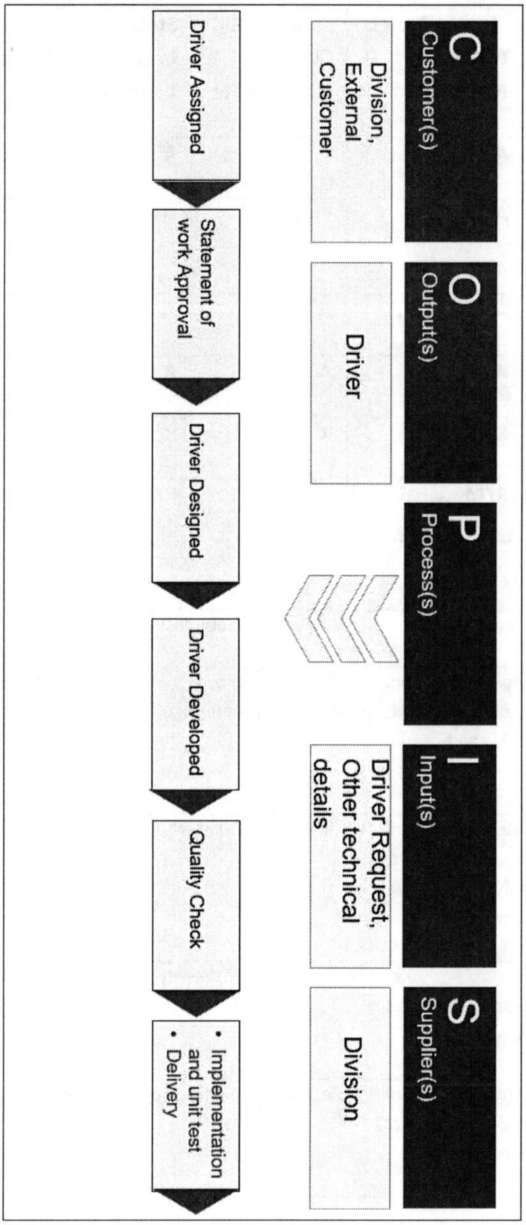

c) Create ARMI and Communication Plan

Stakeholders	Step 1: Project Purpose & Background	Step 2-4: Current & Future State	Step 5-8: Solution Implementation & Control
(Project Sponsor)	A	I	A
(Project Champion)	A	I	A
(MBB)	A	A	A
(Business Leader)	A	A	A
(Project Lead)	R	R	R
(Project Team)	R/M	R/M	R/M

Event	Message	Audience	Frequency	Responsibility	Medium
Project Team Meeting	Update of work done on the project. Identify and agree on next steps.	A, R, I	Monthly	Project Lead	Meeting (Face to Face)
Stakeholder Review	Update of work done on the project. Identify and agree on next steps.	A, R, I	Quarterly	Project Lead	Web-ex
Lean Checkpoint Review	Discuss Lean methodology and process.	A, R, I	Bi-Weekly	Project Lead	Meeting (Face to Face)
Project Update	Update of work done on the project and next steps.	A, R, I, M	Weekly	Project Lead	Email

Step 2: Create Data Collection Plan

Define Measures		Operational Definition	Data collection		
What is to be measured?	**Data type**	**Definition/Formula**	**Who**	**When**	**Source**
No of drivers shipped	Discrete	Total drivers released	Project Lead	9-Jul 20**	Tracking sheet
No of drivers on time	Discrete	Drivers released on or before the committed release date	Project Lead	9-Jul 20**	Tracking sheet
OTD %	Discrete	Total drivers released on-time in % = (No. of drivers on-time/ No. of drivers shipped) * 100	Project Lead	9-Jul 20**	Tracking sheet
Delay reasons – internal	Discrete	Delay Reasons at development team's end	Project Lead	15-Jul 20**	Tracking sheet
Delay reasons – External	Discrete	Delay Reasons at division's end	Project Lead	25-Jul 20**	Tracking sheet

Step 3: Draw Current State Value Stream Map and Identify Kaizens

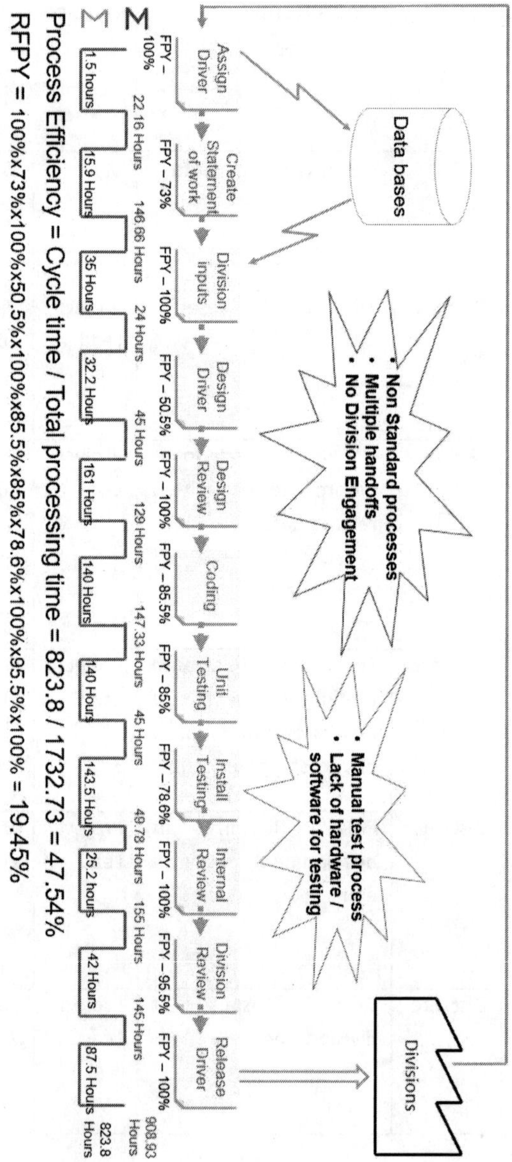

In this VSM the process efficiency is at 47.54% and rolled first pass yield (RFPY) is at 19.45% only. This indicates lot of non-value-added activities and rework are happening in the process.

Step 4: Identify the cause of driver delay with the help of fish bone diagram

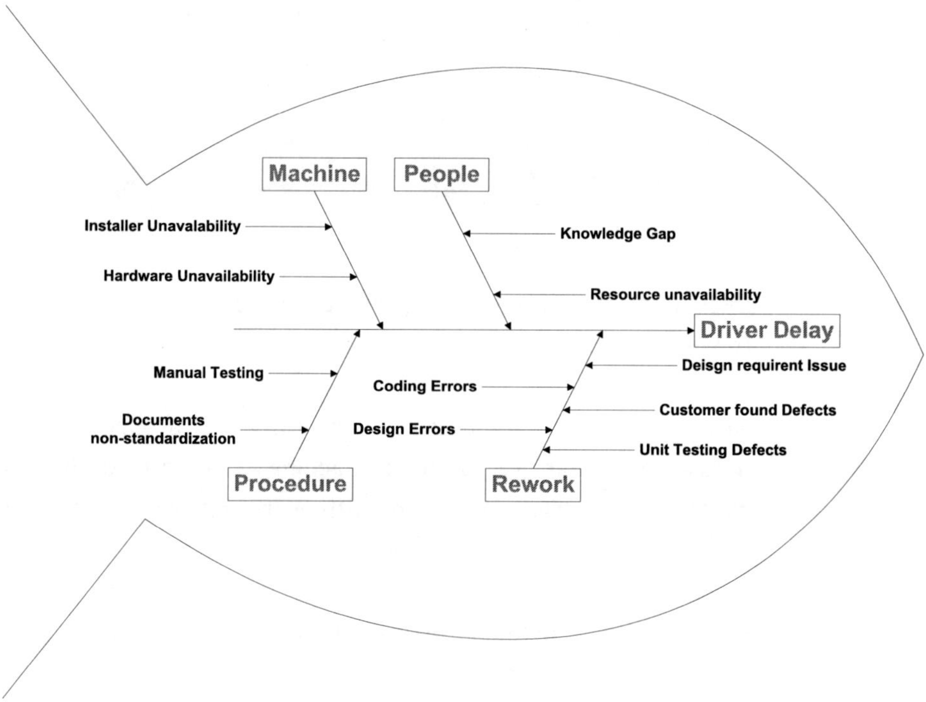

1. Rework: With the help of pareto, top 20% of the causes were identified which were contributing to the 75% of the rework in the process.

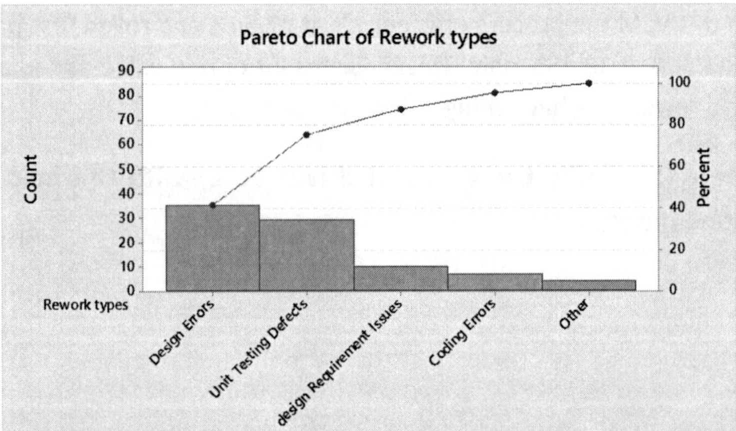

Count	35	29	10	7	4
Percent	41.2	34.1	11.8	8.2	4.7
Cum %	41.2	75.3	87.1	95.3	100.0

Design Errors and Unit testing defects were major cause of the rework

2. Machine: To solve for these issues of installer availability and hardware availability, a build machine was created. It will automatically build the installer with every improving version of the software. It will virtually get the hardware required for the driver development.
3. Procedure: For manual testing, an auto-testing solution was build and all the process documents were standardized.
4. People: Training program was created to upskill the resources and Heijunka concepts of lean were used to eliminate Muda, Muri and Mura. Cross team utilization solved the resource unavailability issue. Resource engagement with Division was resolved by setting up governance structure

Step 5. The team then did data analysis to find out the contributing causes to the problem.

First they collected data on 85 drivers and did statistical analysis, which is listed below:

S.No	Driver cycle time	Installer availability	Auto testing	Hardware availability
1	1827.973	N	No	No
2	1690.957	Y	No	Yes
3	1840.201	N	No	No
4	1801.135	N	No	No
5	1595.688	Y	Yes	Yes
6	1728.839	N	No	No
7	1807.137	N	No	No
8	1579.29	Y	Yes	Yes
9	1769.79	N	No	Yes
10	1861.797	N	No	No
11	1638.675	Y	Yes	No
12	1633.998	Y	No	No
13	1674.216	Y	No	No
14	1665.715	Y	Yes	No
15	1904.286	N	No	No

16	1542.792	Y	Yes	Yes
17	1752.654	N	No	Yes
18	1794.49	N	No	No
19	1787.258	N	No	No
20	1632.619	Y	Yes	No
21	1686.083	Y	No	Yes
22	1918.376	N	No	No
23	1869.956	N	No	No
24	1757.917	N	No	Yes
25	1599.086	Y	Yes	Yes
26	1652.023	Y	Yes	No
27	1723.69	N	No	No
28	1513.771	Y	Yes	Yes
29	1635.37	Y	Yes	No
30	1711.087	N	No	No
31	1651.037	N	Yes	No
32	1750.769	N	No	Yes
33	1805.427	N	No	No
34	1745.49	N	No	No
35	1572.452	Y	Yes	Yes
36	1705.793	Y	No	Yes

37	1723.949	N	No	No
38	1779.946	N	No	No
39	1769.087	N	No	Yes
40	1586.018	Y	Yes	Yes
41	1853.375	N	No	No
42	1593.027	Y	Yes	Yes
43	1840.652	N	No	No
44	1628.875	Y	Yes	No
45	1699.366	Y	No	Yes
46	1678.302	Y	No	Yes
47	1620.541	Y	Yes	No
48	1724.991	N	No	No
49	1716.821	N	No	No
50	1707.083	N	No	Yes
51	1765.003	N	No	Yes
52	1889.204	N	No	No
53	1669.04	Y	No	No
54	1771.969	N	No	Yes
55	1636.865	Y	Yes	No
56	1895.323	N	No	No
57	1795.754	N	No	No

58	1747.566	N	No	No
59	1752.363	N	No	Yes
60	1639.273	Y	Yes	No
61	1803.149	N	No	No
62	1732.252	N	No	No
63	1834.032	N	No	No
64	1788.473	N	No	No
65	1745.225	N	No	No
66	1780.816	N	No	No
67	1803.515	N	No	No
68	1776.183	N	No	Yes
69	1811.973	N	No	No
70	1620.156	Y	Yes	Yes
71	1558.972	Y	Yes	Yes
72	1587.461	Y	Yes	Yes
73	1669.025	Y	Yes	No
74	1656.507	Y	Yes	No
75	1572.215	Y	Yes	Yes
76	1944.056	N	No	No
77	1652.744	Y	Yes	No
78	1663.071	Y	Yes	No

79	1738.371	N	No	No
80	1765.15	N	No	Yes
81	1661.177	Y	Yes	No
82	1706.74	N	No	Yes
83	1828.845	N	No	No
84	1898.15	N	No	No
85	1779.696	N	No	No

First step was to identify the normality of the data and Minitab output shows P value of 0.667, indicating data is normal.

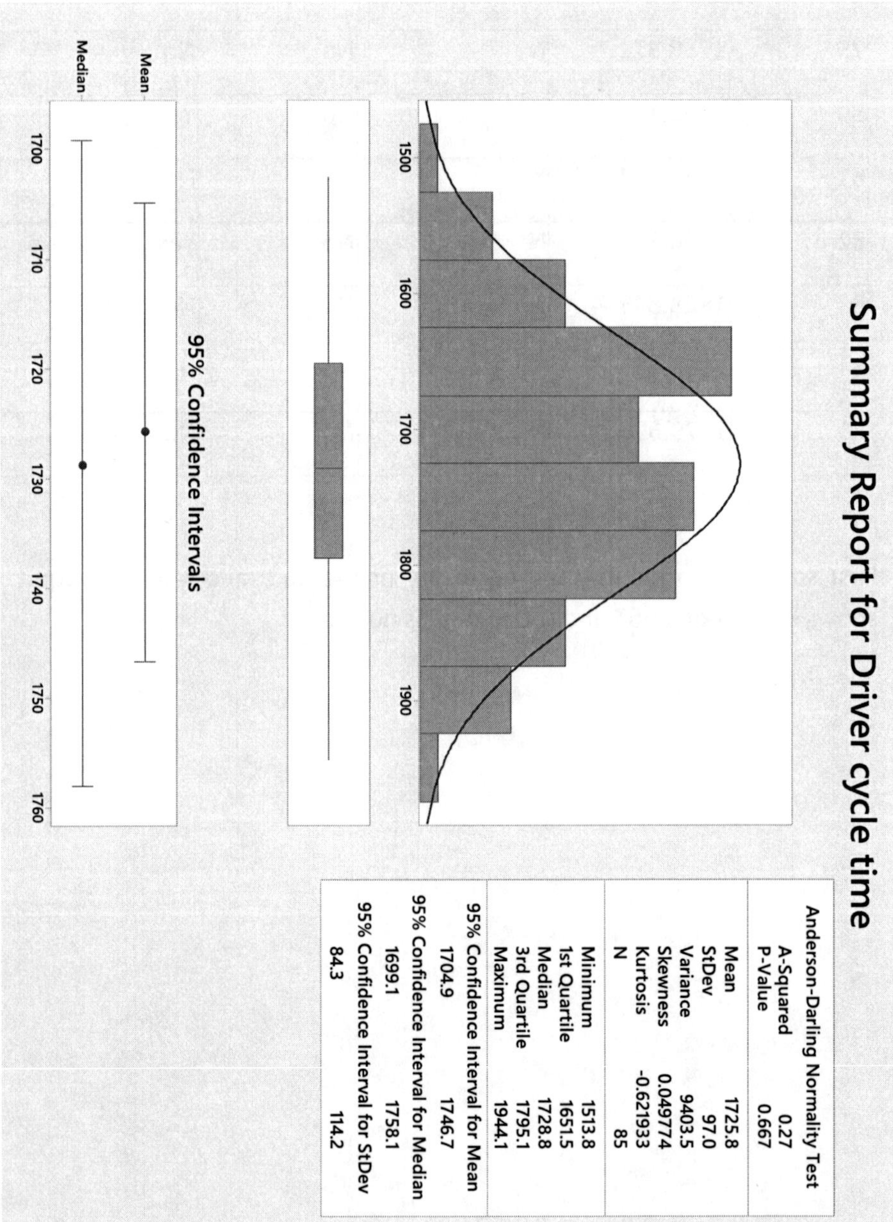

Second step was to identify significant causes through hypothesis testing:

One-way ANOVA: Driver cycle time versus Installer availability

Method

Null hypothesis	All means are equal
Alternative hypothesis	At least one mean is different
Significance level	α = 0.05

Equal variances were assumed for the analysis.

Factor Information

Factor	Levels	Values
Installer availability	2	N, Y

Analysis of Variance

Source	DF	Adj SS	Adj MS	F-Value	P-Value
Installer availability	1	522532	522532	162.22	0.000
Error	83	267360	3221		
Total	84	789892			

Since P value of this test is 0, it indicates Installer unavailability is a significant cause of driver cycle time.

One-way ANOVA: Driver cycle time versus Auto testing

Method

Null hypothesis	All means are equal
Alternative hypothesis	At least one mean is different
Significance level	α = 0.05

Equal variances were assumed for the analysis.

Factor Information

Factor	Levels	Values
Auto testing	2	No, Yes

Analysis of Variance

Source	DF	Adj SS	Adj MS	F-Value	P-Value
Auto testing	1	479191	479191	128.01	0.000
Error	83	310700	3743		
Total	84	789892			

Since P value of this test is 0, it indicates auto testing is a significant cause to driver cycle time.

This is how all the causes were tested and new solution development happened for all significant causes.

Step 6: Kaizen identification and implementation (Solution)

Kaizen 1: Resolving people issues

Problem Kaizen	• Low / No Engagement with divisions. • Quality assurance resource from Division was not allocated as per the committed schedule. • Formal communication on the project progress was missing. • Governance structure was missing. • Resources unavailability to develop drivers

Identifying resources by cross training and bandwidth comparison using time & motion study

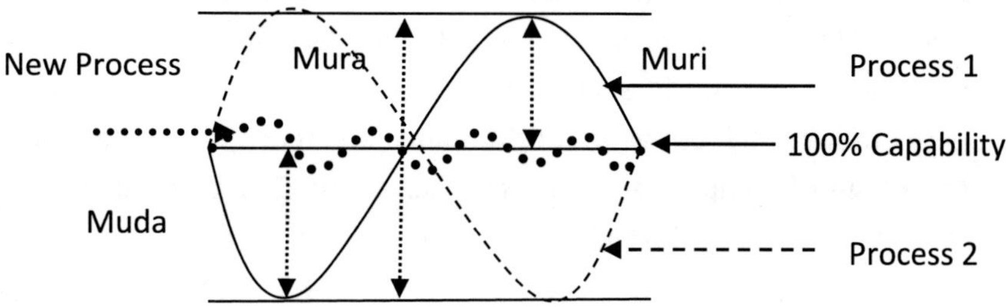

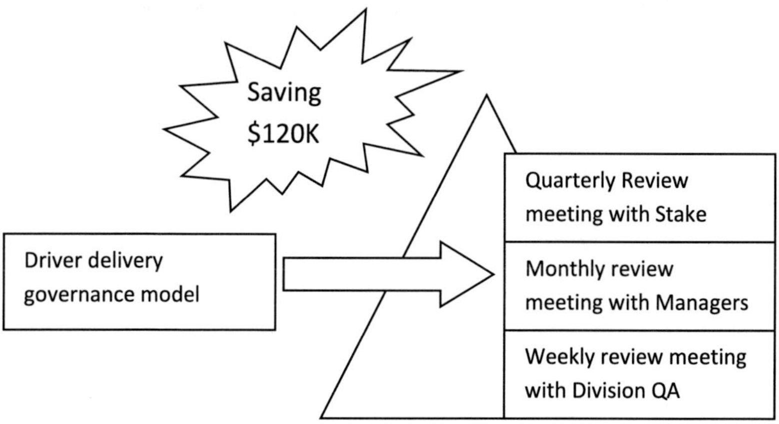

Solution Kaizen:

The team improved the driver development communication & division engagement model. This was done by getting the requirement documents upfront which led to reducing the rework in the design phase due to change in inputs.

Time and motion study were conducted to understand the bandwidth of the resources working in different teams, resources were identified and trained by comparing 2 process together. Concepts of Heijunka were used for load leveling and sequencing of the work done.

After doing team capacity utilization through time and motion study, two teams - acorn and pine, having similar kind of work were studied together. At any given point in time, teams had MUDA as waiting waste time corresponding to other team having Muri (overburdened) at the same time. We used Heijunka concept of sequencing and load leveling to resolve this issue. Acorn team was developing difficult drivers in Week 1, Medium Complex in week 2-3 and easy drivers in week 4. The work was sequenced in such a manner that driver development was distributed evenly between both teams and each team had equal percentage of complex and easy reconciliations. The work load of the teams was balanced through the cross functional training program and utilizing resources wherever needed. By implementing the standardization concept of Hejunka, standard process documents were created for all the processes

Kaizen 2: Procedure (Manual Testing and Non-Standard documentation)

Problem Kaizen	• All the install tests were conducted manually which took a lot of time since these tests are to be conducted on different operating systems. • Al the process documents were nonstandard.

Manual and Non-Standard Process	***Automated Standardized Process***
Reimage the test machine for desired OS	Automated tool reimage test machine for desired OS
↓	↓
Manual Installation testing	Auto installation test
↓	↓
Verify Driver and create test report	Auto verify the driver & generate auto test report
↓	↓
Fill the driver release checklist	High level test report generation & auto email to developers

Solution Kaizen:

The automated & standardized test process reimages the machine to desired Operating System, installs the prerequisite software's & run the installation tests as per the checklist without any human intervention required once the test is triggered. It generates a pass/fail test summary report for all the tests conducted on each operating system. This report is automatically emailed to the intended recipients to verify the results.

Kaizen 3: Machine (Installer Unavailability and Hardware Unavailability)

Problem Kaizen	• Every time a new version of the driver software is generated, manual installer creation was a time-consuming activity • To test the software locally the hardware was not available

Saving $90K

Manual Installer Creation	Build infrastructure was created to auto create the installer
Hardware unavailab ility	Simulator / Emulator was created to create a copy of the hardware required

Solution Kaizen:

To eliminate the manual creation of installer, the team created build infrastructure which automatically created the installer (every new software which is download has to be installed separately, so installer are required to install the software)

Emulator was designed by the team to create a copy of the hardware required for testing the software.

Kaizen 4: Rework

All the causes of the rework were identified, and a Pareto chart was created to identify top 20% causes which contribute to 75% of the rework.

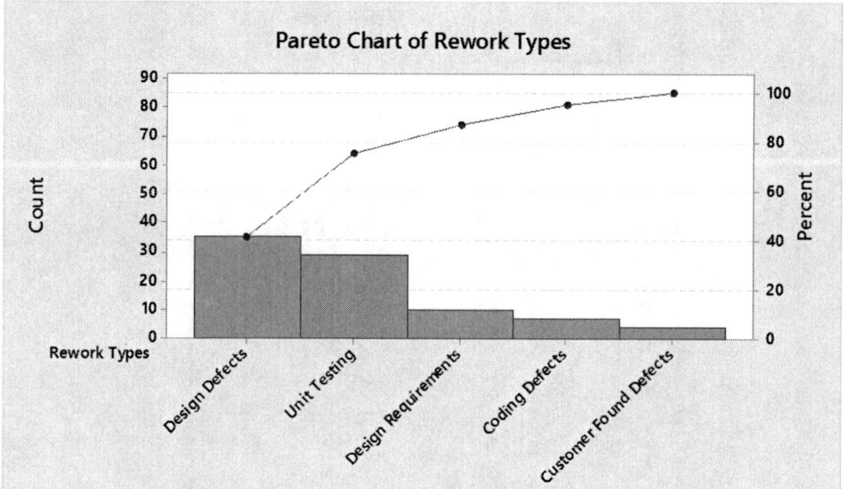

Count	35	29	10	7	4
Percent	41.2	34.1	11.8	8.2	4.7
Cum %	41.2	75.3	87.1	95.3	100.0

A training was developed which helped reduce the Design and Unit testing defects

Step 7:

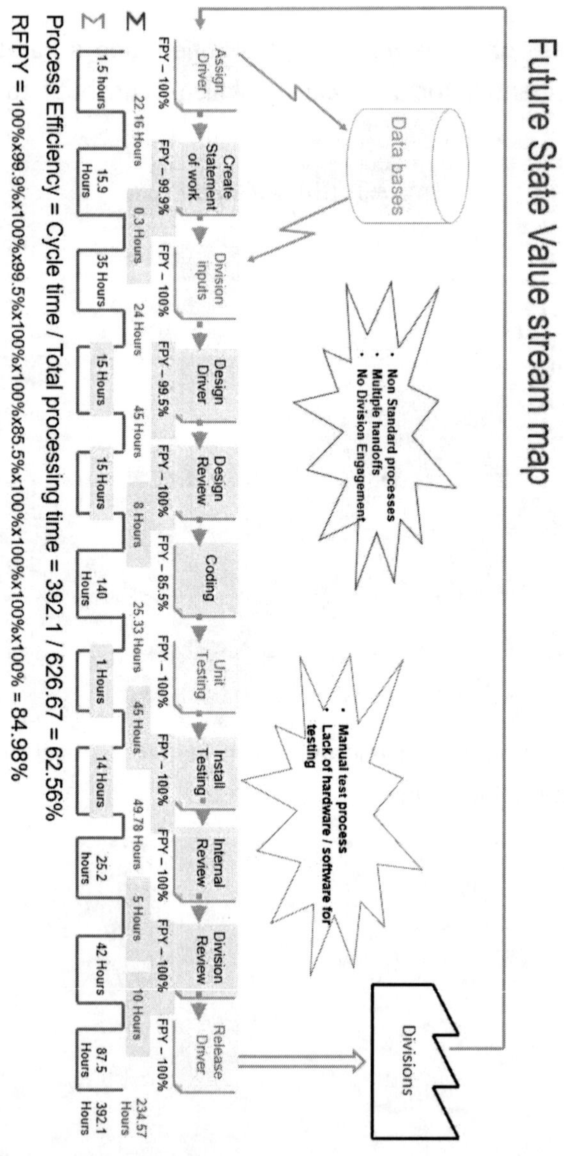

Process efficiency has improved from 47.54% to 62.56%

Rolled first pass yield has improved from 19.45% to 84.98%

b) Create a Solution Implementation plan

What is to be implemented	**Where it is to be implemented**	**Who will implement**	**By When**	**How it is to be implemented**
Checkpoint meeting with division	Web-ex (Weekly)	Developer	7-Sep **	Developer sets up a meeting
Technical trainings	Class room session	Team Lean	14-Sep **	Quarterly classroom sessions
Build machine update	Lab	Team Lead	5 –Oct **	Develop automated build definition
Test Automation	Test scripts	Developer	12 – Oct **	Develop new test scripts

Before implementing the solutions, Failure Mode & Effect Analysis was done to identify any failure modes due to changes suggested. Where ever the RPN score was more than 100, a mitigation plan was prepared and executed so that there were no failures post solution implementation.

d) Create Failure Mode and Effect Analysis

Potential Failure mode	Severity	Potential Cause of Failure	Occurrence	Current process control	Detection	RPN	Recommended actions
Incomplete requirement	8	Improper/ Lack of communication	7	Questions to division sent for details.	7	392	Close loop with division and introduces regular checkpoint meetings.
Scope Changes	8	Division priorities changes.	8	No control.	9	576	
Design review not done on time.	8	Resource not available.	2	Follow up with division and checkpoint meeting	5	80	
Instrument access unavailable.	8	Instrument FW not ready or not stabilize.	5	Follow up with division.	5	200	Introduce weekly meeting with Division resource.
Instrument setting not available.	8	LP is not complete.	5	Ask to domain expert.	5	200	Meeting with domain expert.
Less number of model available.	8	Instrument not available for testing	8	No control.	8	512	Make a high-level test plan to prioritize instrument models.

Step 8: Pre and Post analysis

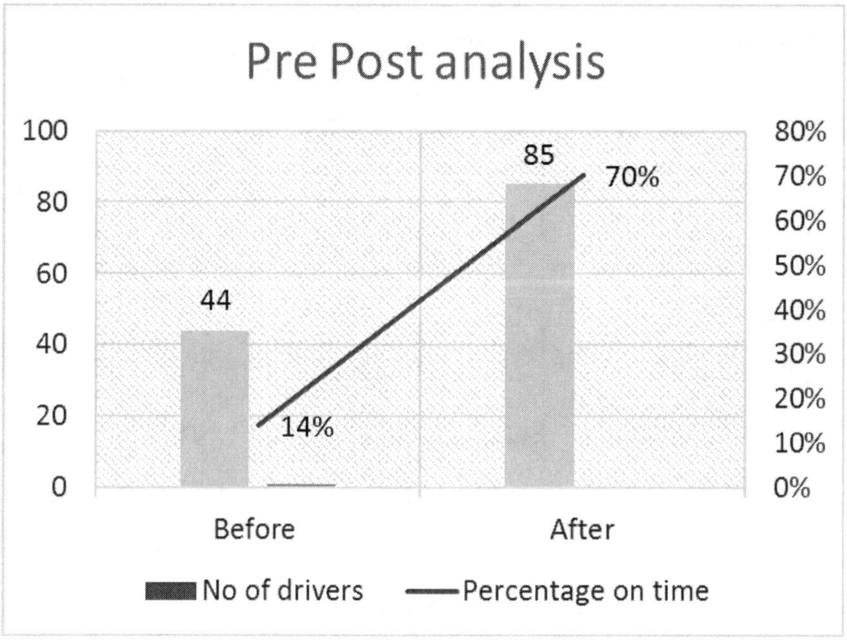

The graph above shows that before the project, the team had 14% on-time delivery and developed only 44 drivers in last 6 months. However after the project, they were able to develop 85 drivers with 70% on time delivery.

Step 8: Control Plan

What is to be implemented	Where it is to be implemented	Who will implement	How it is to be implemented	Frequency of check	Checked by
Checkpoint meeting with division	Web-ex (Weekly)	Each developer	Developer sets up a meeting	Fortnightly	Manager
Build machine	Lab	Team Lead	Develop automated build definition	Weekly	Manager
Test Automation	Test scripts	Team Lead	Develop new test scripts	Weekly	Manager

Control plan is created to check that improved state is always under control and older problems don't reoccur.

Step 8: Benefit realization

Annual impact	
Drivers Before Project	44
Drivers after project	85
Total Additional drivers developed	41
Total additional resources required to develop extra Drivers	12

Realized Savings: $ 360K	
Annual Cost of 1 Engineer in India	$ 30K
Total Cost of Resources saved (annual)	$ 360K

With the improvements in place, the team is able to achieve 128% more amount of work with the same number of resources, leading to the resource savings of $ 360K

Case Study 4: Reduce loan approval cycle time

In a call centre, cycle time to process a loan application is a big problem. ABC bank takes too much time to approve personal loans for their customers. It has been observed that the leads generated by the call center are lost to the competition due to time taken by the bank to approve the loans. The rejection rate of the loan applications is also very high.

Only approx. 40% of the loan applications are passed in first go and processing a filled loan application till approval takes more than 400 minutes. This is huge time compared to competition.

Step 1: Create VOC/VOB chart

Business – Internal Management			Customer – Bank's Customers		
Voice of Business	**Business Issues**	**Critical business requirement**	**Critical customer requirement**	**Customer Issues**	**Voice of Customer**
Personal loan approval is time consumin g process	Loose customer base to competition due to high cycle time for loan approval	Reduce cycle time for personal loan approval process	Personal loan should be approved in less than 2 hours	Personal Loan approval takes lot of time	Loan approval is a time taking process
CTQ / CTP – To reduce the loan approval cycle time from 417 minutes to 90 minutes					

As customer and business are demanding the reduction in loan approval cycle time, so the goal of the project was considered on the same.

b) Next step is to create a project charter

Business Case

ABC bank takes too much time to approve personal loans for their customers. It has been observed that the leads generated by the call center are lost to the competition due to time taken by the bank to approve the loans. The rejection rate of the loan applications is also very high.

Only approx. 40% of the loan applications are passed in first go and processing a filled loan application till approval takes more than 400 minutes. This is huge time compared to competition.

Scope

In scope – Personal loans

Out of scope – All other loan types

Problem Statement

Observed over the last 3 months data cycle time to process loan application is high with close to 35% of rejection rate.

Milestones

	Start date	End date
Step 1	15 Jun **	30 Jun **
Step 2,3,4	1 Jul **	20 Aug **
Step 5,6,7	21 Aug **	3o Oct **
Step 8	01 Nov **	31 Dec **

Goal Statement

To reduce the loan approval cycle time from 417 minutes to 90 minutes by Dec 20**

Team charter

Champion: Process VP
Sponsor: Customer VP
Mentor: Master Black Belt
Process Owner: Process Manager
Team Members: M1 & M2

I am not repeating the common slides like SIPOC, ARMI chart & Communication plan as they are similar in all the case studies.

Step 2: Next important step is to create a data collection plan

Define Measures		Operational Definition		Data collection		
What is to be measured?	**Data type**	**Definition**	**Formula Used**	**Where**	**When**	**How**
Loan approval rate	Binary discrete	No of loan approved by the bank	Total approvals / total applications	Excel template	07 Jul 20**	Collect data from day end system report
Cycle time data at each step	Continuous	Time taken to process each step	No formula	On the floor	8 Jul 20**	Sit with the processors and record live
Calculate FPY at each Process step	Discrete	Total work without rework	Total correct output without rework / Total input	Excel template	10 Jul 20**	Do a sample-based audit and upload information

Step 3: Create current state value stream map

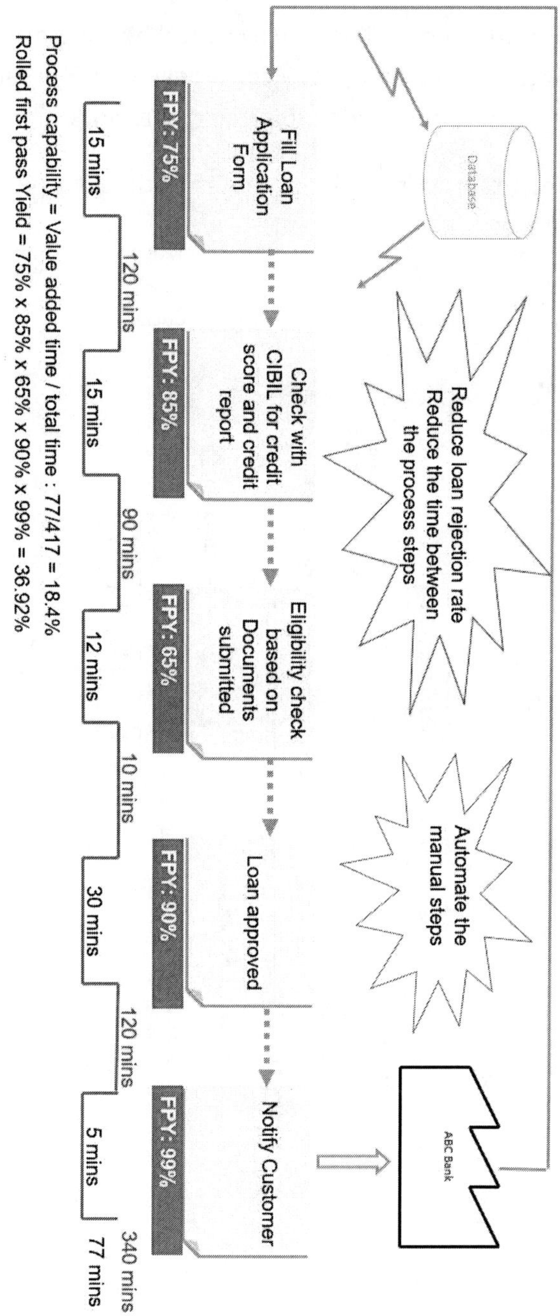

In this Value stream map, it is very evident that the process capability is only 18.4% and Rolled first pass yield is only 36.92% - implying 63.08% of the loan applications needed some kind of rework.

It is also important to identify the causes of the high cycle time of lean approval process.

Step 3: Identification of causes

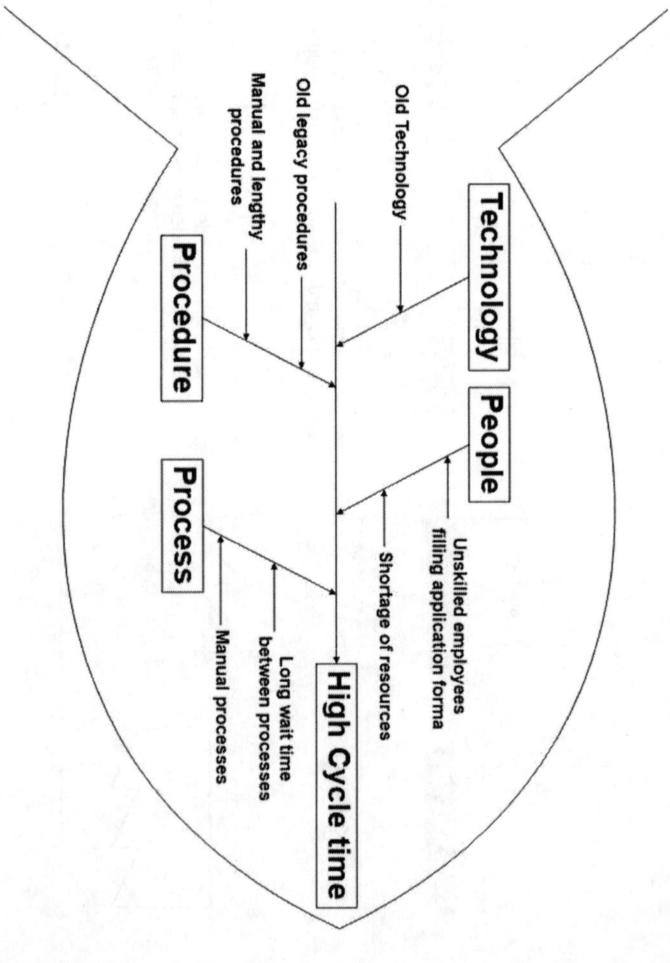

Step 4: The next step is to identify the future state of the process

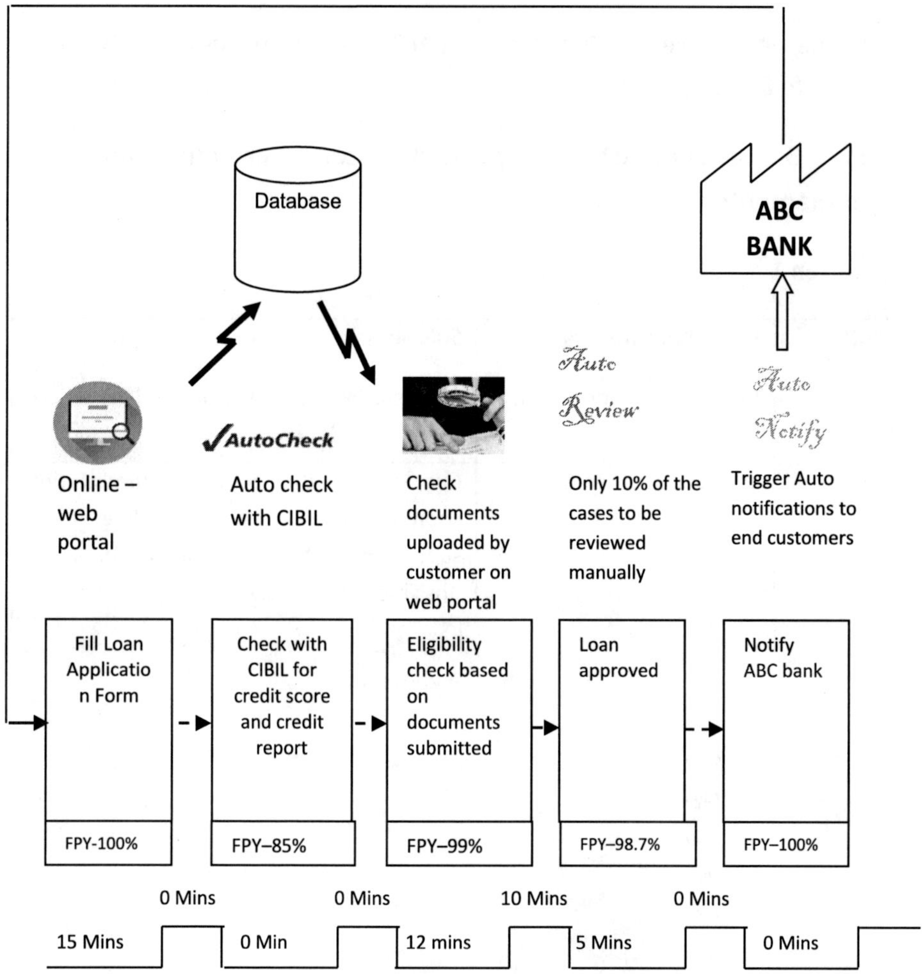

Process capability = Value added time / total time: 32/42 = 76.2%

Rolled first pass Yield = 100% x 85% x 99% x 98.7% x 100% = 83.05%

The future state of the process shows various solution implementation at each step of the process which includes creation of web portal, mobile app and various process automations.

In the new process, the process capability will increase to 76.2% and RFPY to 83.05%.

Step 5 & 6: Some of the important Kaizens were identified and implemented:

Kaizen 1:

S.No	**Rejection category**	**Solution**
1	Incomplete Information	Create a Web portal where all fields are made mandatory
2	Lack of Documents	Checklist of the entire documentation should be available online and submission of form should only be possible with attachments.

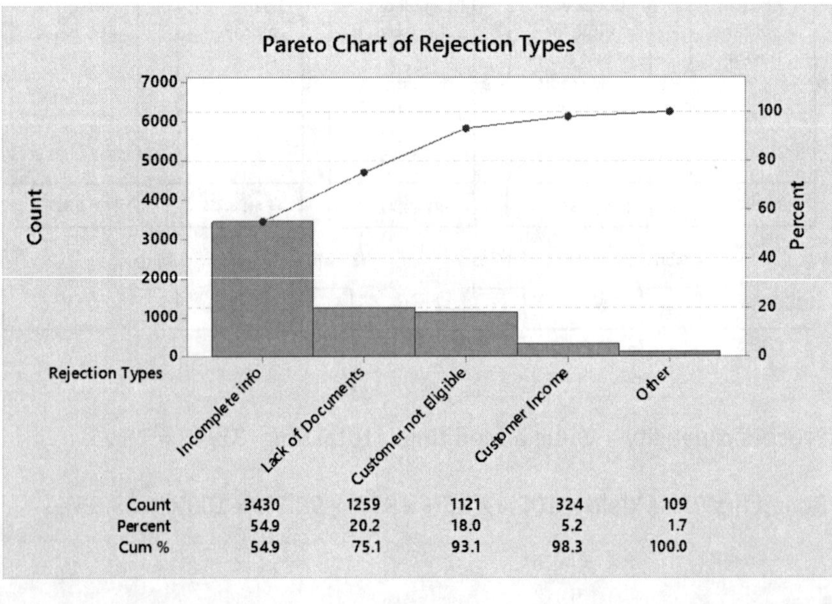

Kaizen 2:

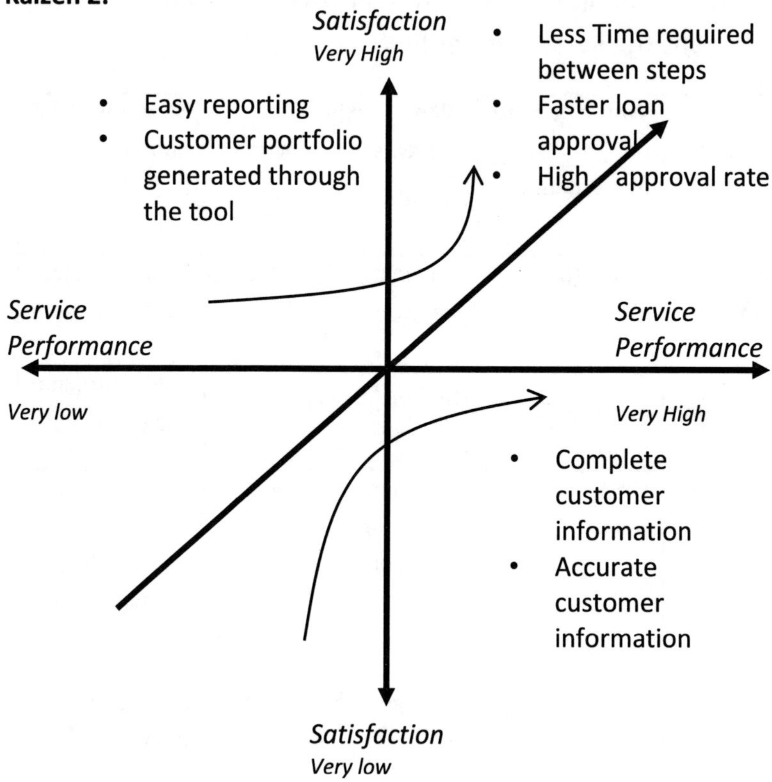

Kano Model

Kano survey was conducted to identify and classify customer requirements (internal customers).

All the requirements were classified into

- Must have
- Satisfiers
- Delighter

Must be requirements are complete & accurate customer Information.

Satisfier are Less time between process steps, Faster loan approvals through the tool, & high approval rate.

Delighters are easy reporting & generation of customer portfolio from the tool

Step 7: Solution implementation plan was formed and executed to implement the kaizens identified.

What is to be implemented	Where it is to be implemented	Who will implement	By When	How it is to be implemented
Training to the field staff	Board room	Training manager	7-Oct **	Train Field staff on new tool and hand-held terminal usage
Creation of Web ex portal	On Web ex portal	Information technology manager	14-Oct **	Get the requirement and use Scrum methodology
Creation of mobile application	IT Lab	IT team manager	25 – Oct **	Develop a mobile app for field team

Step 8: Failure mode and effect analysis is conducted on all the possible failure modes to identify the potential failures and to mitigate them.

Process / Function	Potential Failure mode	Potential Effect of failure	Severity	Potential Cause of Failure	Occurrence	Current process control	Detection	RPN	Recommended actions
Web Portal	Not functioning	Delay in Loan application submission	8	Too much load on website	7	No back up servers	7	392	Create back up servers for the Web portal
Web Portal	Slow	Delay in Loan App Submission	6	Network not proper	8	No control.	9	432	Make sure the applications are filled on by using LAN cable
Mobile app	Not working on iPhone	iPhone users will not be able to use	7	App is not adaptable to iPhone	6	No control	9	378	Create an app for iPhone users also

All the Failure modes where RPN score is greater than 100 are identified and an improvement plan is put in place to get these RPN scores to less than 100.

Step 8: Pre and Post assessment

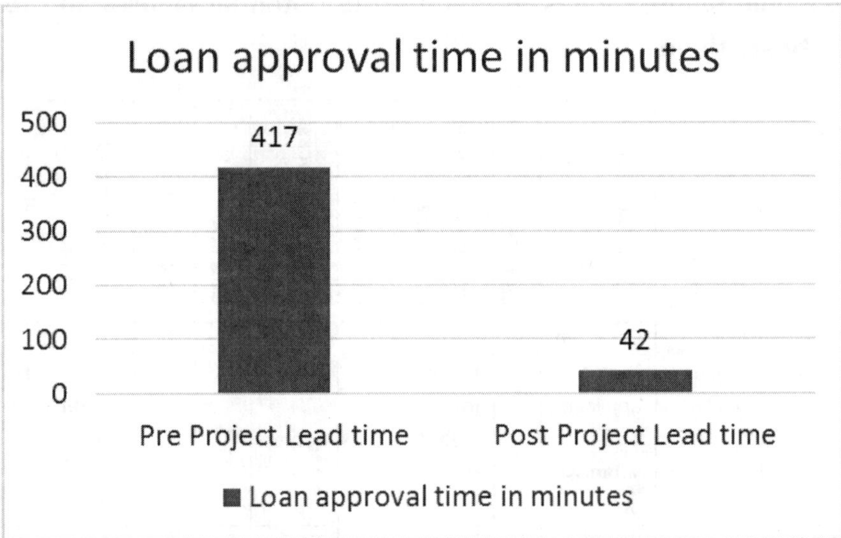

Loan approval time has been reduced from 417 Minutes to 42 minutes against a goal of 90 Minutes.

Step 8: Pre and Post assessment

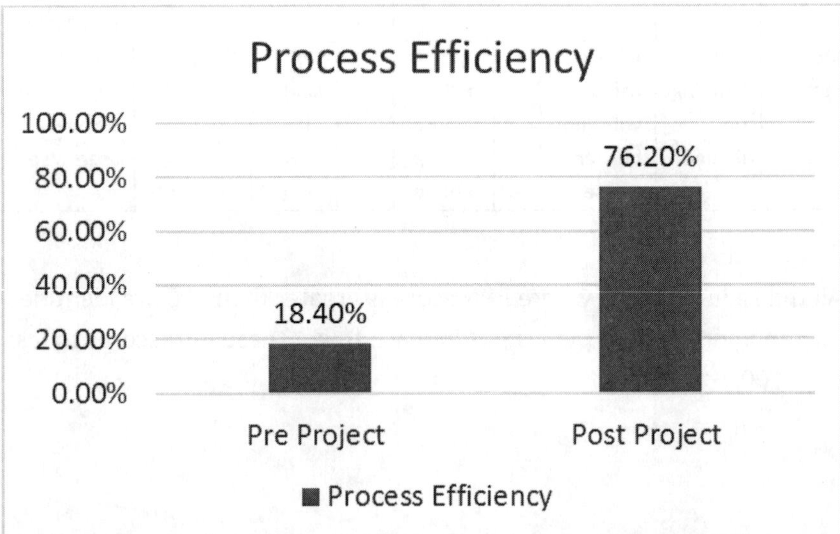

Process efficiency has been improved from 18.4% to 76.20%.

Last but not the least, the Pre-post analysis of the project is performed, and radical improvements are noticed. This project has made huge tangible and non-tangible impacts - tangible impact of $50 Mn and non-tangible impact of positive movement in customer satisfaction score from 8 to 9.7.

Lean Facilitation Guide:

Building a Lean six sigma DNA in an organisation is an integral part of the work that needs to be done as an ongoing initiative. Every Lean Six Sigma project that gets certified must be evaluated across a minimum of three levels.

The 8-Stage Lean project should be evaluated and reviewed at Step 1, Step 4 and Step 8

A Lean facilitator should be actively involved in project reviews right from the predefine stage, asking focused questions on the team construct. Some typical, useful questions to ensure team success are:

- Who is the assigned Champion and Sponsor for the team?
- What training have the team members and the Black Belt had?
- Have all team members been trained on lean tools and methodology?
- How much time does the Champion spend with your team?
- How often does the team meet?
- What is the percentage of attendance at meetings?
- How much time do members spend outside of meetings working on the project?
- Are there barriers for collaboration within the team? If so, what plans are there to address them?
- When did the project start? When is the planned completion date? Is the project on schedule?
- How is the team tracking and documenting its accomplishments?
- What other resources does the team need to assure success?

Step 1 Review:

Define the customer, their CTQs, the team charter and the business process.

Some of the critical must dos for this phase are:

- Customers to be identified and segmented as required. Data to verify customers' needs and requirements needs to be collected and plotted.
- A written team charter that includes rationale for project, preliminary problem statement, scope, goals, milestones, and roles and responsibilities.
- Completed and validated high level 'as is' process map (COPIS) which identifies customer, output, five to seven process blocks of activities, inputs and suppliers.

Some tools which can help in this phase are:

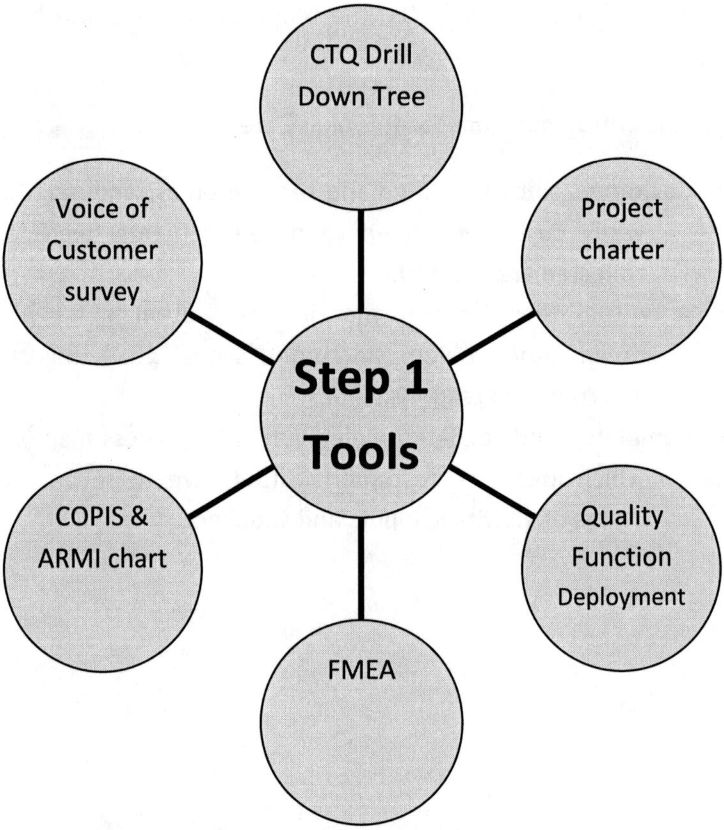

Some of the Dos and Don'ts for this phase are:

Do	Don't
The metric should be selected on the smallest unit of the process, because if the smallest unit is set right, the entire process is bound to be right. Work on direct metric not on derived metric.	Avoid dollar value as a metric, like reducing the day's sales outstanding (DSO) \$30 K per day to \$25 K per day. Use business impact to highlight dollar values and impact. Always choose metrics like improving hit rates of calls from 25% to 45%, hence reducing DSO. In this example, the business impact could be a DSO reduction of \$5 K per day.
Pick up the actual cause of customers' problems as the project metric. Customers will always give you a practical problem; convert it to a statistical statement. E.g.: Practical problem: I am not happy with the process quality. Statistical problem: To reduce the number of defects from 20% to 5% by April 2012.	Do not take project metrics for which you cannot collect accurate or complete data. Metrics that are complex and difficult need to be explained to others. Metrics that complicate operations and create excessive overhead. Metrics that cause employees to act not in the best interests of the business but just to 'meet their numbers'.
Business case must have 'what for and why' this project is required, apart from the background of the process.	Not more than one problem statement for one project.
Slide on business impact calculation and replication projects.	
Customer signs off emails on business impact approach and charter.	

Step 2-4 review:

This review is for evaluating and reviewing Steps 2, 3 and 4.

Step 2: Identify Process Steps, prepare data collection plan and Collect Data*

Lean Facilitator should help the team define the process steps and then help them identify the right sample size to collect data. The best sampling technique is Stratified random sampling.

Stratified Sampling: Different groups of similar characteristics are made based on location, occupation, complexity or age. Then a random sample is taken from each group proportional to the size of each group. It leads to very good random representative sample. For example, if the sample of 60 is to be picked from 1000 (Simple, medium and high complexity) transactions, than 3 different clusters are made - First cluster representing Simple complexity transactions (500), Second cluster representing Medium complexity transactions (250) and third cluster representing high complexity transactions (250). Then randomly 30 transactions should be picked from Simple complexity transaction's clusters and 15 each from the other two clusters.

Data Collection & Current performance on Key Performance Metrics (Collect at least 5 days of data prior to the LEAN event or minimum of 30 sample size)

Step 3: Document current state

Lean Facilitator must help the project lead in documenting the current state of the process. They should help the team in identifying wastes at all the steps of the value stream. Waste walk can also be done to identify wastes.

Team should be able to identify cycle time and wait time at each step. They should also be able to identify inventory and first pass yield at all the steps.

Lean facilitator must be able to guide the team on how to collect data on cycle time like how many samples at what time should be monitored.

As a thumb rule inventory samples at different process steps are to be recorded at beginning, afternoon and evening. Then average out these numbers to find out average inventory at each process step. There could be another way to record this. However the facilitator must finalize these at the start of VSM and write the guidelines upfront.

Step 4: Lean Facilitator must be present when future state VSM is created and all Kaizens are identified.

Some of the tools used in this phase are

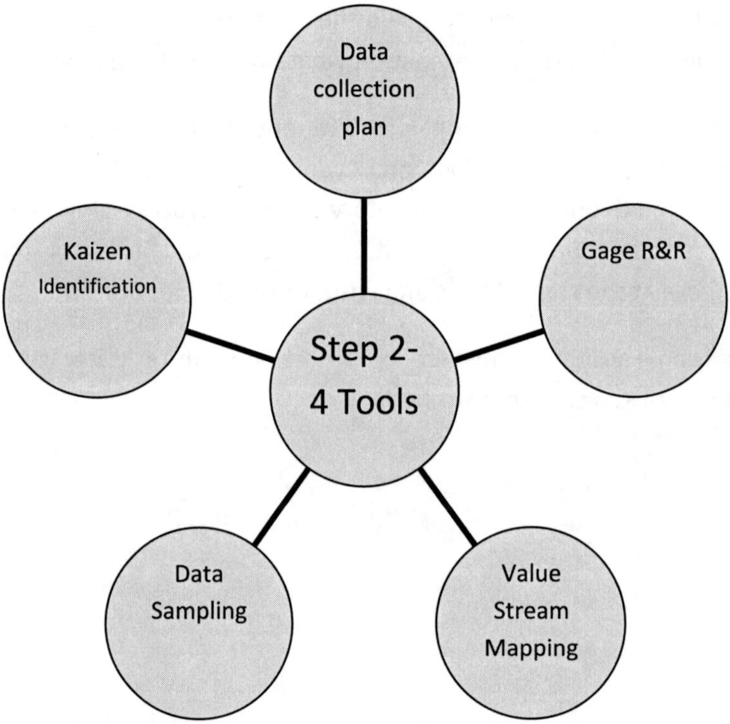

Do	Don't
Data collection plan should be prepared before team starts data collection.	Collect abstract data
Stratified random sampling	No sampling technique
Use sample calculator to identify statistically significant sample.	Use a good % of sample size

Step 5-8 Review:

This review is for evaluating and reviewing Steps 5, 6, 7 and 8.

Step 5: Prioritize the Kaizen by using control impact metrics or cause and effect metrics.

Step 6: Data analysis for key causes should be facilitated and team should be helped in identifying key causes with the help of data. Some of the key causes are Inventory, Cycle Time, Defect Rate / Yield, Volumes, No. Of Operators.

Step 7: Action workout and Implementation: Lean facilitator must help the team in implementing the key kaizens, they should also help the team learn as to how to identify the solutions by using lean tools like Heijunka, Jidokha, 5s, Poka Yoke and Kanban etc.

Step 8: Lean Facilitator must help the team to prepare Pre-Post Metric Comparison, Control Plan & Benefit Realization

Some of the tools used in this phase are

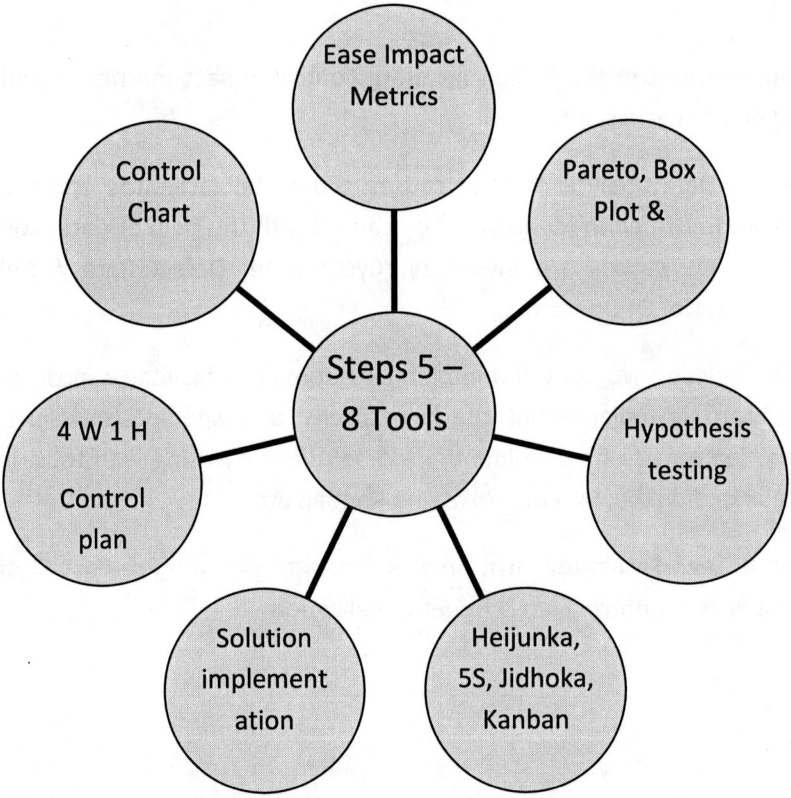